My Brother *My Sister*

ALSO BY MOLLY HASKELL

From Reverence to Rape: The Treatment of Women in the Movies

Love and Other Infectious Diseases: A Memoir

Holding My Own in No Man's Land:
Women and Men and Films and Feminists

Frankly, My Dear: Gone with the Wind *Revisited*

MOLLY HASKELL

My Brother *My Sister*

Story of a Transformation

VIKING

VIKING
Published by the Penguin Group
Penguin Group (USA) Inc., 375 Hudson Street,
New York, New York 10014, USA

USA I Canada I UK I Ireland I Australia I New Zealand I India I South Africa I China
Penguin Books Ltd, Registered Offices: 80 Strand, London WC2R 0RL, England
For more information about the Penguin Group visit penguin.com

LIBRARY OF CONGRESS CATALOGING-IN-PUBLICATION DATA
Haskell, Molly.
My brother my sister : story of a transformation / Molly Haskell.
pages cm
ISBN 978-0-670-02552-7
1. Haskell, John Cheves, Jr. 2. Transsexuals—United States—Biography.
3. Sex change—United States—Case studies. I. Title.
HQ77.8.H375 2013
306.76'8092—dc23
[B]   2013016961

Printed in the United States of America
1 3 5 7 9 10 8 6 4 2

Designed by Francesca Belanger
Set in Simoncini Garamond Std

Penguin is committed to publishing works of quality and integrity.
In that spirit, we are proud to offer this book to our readers;
however, the story, the experiences, and the words
are the author's alone.

In memory of our parents, Mary and John Haskell

Contents

Contents

Note to Readers

*I*t is not exactly a spoiler to say that this book got written, though for a while its fate was in doubt. The first thing my brother did was to swear me to silence, both oral and literary. Somewhere along the way, the ban was lifted and I began writing; further along came a cease-and-desist telephone call, and writing was suspended. Eventually, though, he became she, and a deal was struck. She not only agreed to it but participated with generosity and at length. Her words as presented in this book occurred in conversations between us, either in person or over the telephone, both before and after the transition. Once she'd authorized the project, I began recording our conversations, most of which came after she'd undergone the first surgery, facial feminization. However, since many of these discussions occurred in nascent form from the time my sister—then my brother—first told me of her intentions, I have taken the liberty of presenting them in their fuller form from the beginning, to aid the reader in experiencing the story as the two of us experienced it. Although neither my brother/sister's name nor any details or names from our family have been changed, the names of his/her first and second wives and a few other people in his/her immediate family have been altered to protect their privacy. Nevertheless, their words, like my brother/sister's, are their own, and I have presented each person's story as faithfully as I could.

CHAPTER ONE

My Brother Drops a Bombshell

*I*t's the sixth of October, 2005, a crisp Indian summer day in Manhattan, and we're sitting in the dining room of our Upper East Side apartment. Outside the window, against the cobalt blue sky, looms the Church of the Heavenly Rest, where Andrew and I were married, where my brother, tall and handsome in his morning suit, walked me up the aisle and, in my father's stead, gave me away. Now, almost forty years later, he's come alone for a single night, bringing with him a whiff of unease, even alarm. First it was his wife's last-minute cancellation, and now it's the formality with which he's summoned us to the table . . . like one of those scenes from *Law & Order*, when the detectives have to tell the family a loved one is dead.

Named John Cheves Haskell Jr., after our father, he's always been known in the family as Chevey (pronounced "Chivvy" as in "chin"). In addition to being the only immediate family we have (Andrew and I had no children, and Andrew's brother died in a sky-diving accident when he was twenty-eight), Chevey is the one we turn to for help in so many ways—all those areas in which we are inept. From the humbly domestic (What temperature should the refrigerator be? Chevey travels with a special thermometer) to the technological to the arcane ways of money and finance (he's a financial adviser by profession and a rationalist by avocation), my brother is a fixer of problems and a fount of common sense, generous with his time as if there were no end to it. In recent years, the only time I can remember being vexed with him was in this very dining room. Andrew and I were giving a party that required removing a leaf of the chrome and glass table. As Chevey and Eleanor were up visiting, he offered to help remove the panel, but the heavy glass, detached from its chrome frame, dropped and shattered. If Andrew had perpetrated this domestic calamity, it would have been exasperating but unsurprising. At the hands of my hyper-competent brother, it was almost comically out of character. And now he is about to shatter normalcy in our dining room again, in a way that I would have said was out of character if I knew what character was and if character had anything to do with it.

I'm terrified it's some fatal illness, possibly ALS (Lou Gehrig's disease), the degenerative neurological disorder from which our father died. Without our ever talking about it, that possibility has been a constant in our lives. Sensing this, he immediately disposes of it: he's not dying and he doesn't have an illness in the ordinary sense.

"I have what's known as gender dysphoria," he says. "For most of my life, I've felt I should have been born female. And now I'm going to become one."

Stunned silence. Disbelief. How can this be? Chevey, my brother! Andrew's brother-in-law! He's so utterly normal. There's no sudden memory, no flash, no "Of course." He was (and is) a manly guy—no trace of effeminacy or kid in a tutu—who, if not captain of the football team or a hell-raising, beer-swilling male chauvinist, was always plenty virile, and there were two wives who'd have so attested.

When did he know?

"Since way back, early childhood," he tells me, "I had confusing urges, feminine longings, but even in puberty I simply had no concept for what I was experiencing."

"You mean, as the expression has it, a female trapped in a male body?"

"Nothing as clear as that, but just confused feelings, a desire to dress and feel like a girl, not very strong at first."

A desire, it seems, for which neither he nor society had words. His marriages were good, even sexually, but part of every day was increasingly spent in something like agony, imagining himself a woman.

I'm suddenly struck by two odd memories. In the later years of his second marriage, he became anorexic. Eleanor and I kept asking, even nagging, him about it, but he insisted he was doing it to keep his cholesterol down, with his internist's approval.

"I was trying to change my body shape," he now admits.

The other image seems even more telling. For as long as I can remember, he would pick at the skin at his fingertips, almost like an animal gnawing its own flesh, till his fingers became raw.

"I was trying to get out of my skin," he says. And now, in effect, he will.

I think about Eleanor. She has to be devastated. They've had what to all appearances is a wonderful marriage, worked and travelled and built a life together that is about to splinter at the seams. They're separating, he tells me, and eventually he will move to a mountain condo the two of them bought some years ago.

When I ask how she's dealing with it, Chevey's calm voice wavers. "She's having a hard time. I think she's struggling less with the idea of me being transsexual than with losing the marriage. A year and a half before we got married, I told her I had had this problem but I thought I had it under control."

"Why now, at this late date?"

"Because," he explains, "the urge gets stronger, not weaker. You just don't want to go to your grave in what you believe is the wrong body."

I ask him if he ever thought of doing it earlier, if it was the reason he and Beth, his first wife, got divorced. He separated from Beth in 1976. We were all mystified, so joined at the hip were the two. They'd been together since puberty, had dated other people but always come back together.

"Yes, I took hormones," he says. "I was going to change." He bought a charming Tudor house in Richmond's West End and had it rezoned so that it could serve as a financial management consultancy below and residence above.

And then he realized he couldn't do it. Pete, his son with Beth, was still alive, Mother was alive, the doctors he went to presented a confusing picture; there was no Internet, no information, no guidance.

"I didn't anticipate the intensity of the drive. Nobody can imagine it. To the point that not having the sex change is no longer an option. From the outside it looks like a selfish act, but from the inside not at all. I had a 'happy' life before, and I'm destroying it all. It's nothing to do with happiness. I had happiness in all those normal senses.

"It's like . . ." He pauses. "Well, imagine you're a paraplegic, and they tell you they can give you movement in your legs, but you'll have to use a cane. Of course you'd jump at the opportunity. I'll go further," he continues. "I'd rather die in surgery trying to become a woman than live the rest of my life fighting it. The only way I wouldn't go through with the surgery is if there were a 100 percent chance of death."

Spoken in his calm, determined voice, rational to the end, this is so chilling it takes my breath away.

He lays out the plan in his methodical way, precise and logical—the very qualities I love about him and depend on, but that are at odds with the tumultuous event about to unfold and the inner turmoil to which it bears witness. In May he'll have facial reconstruction surgery in California and then move to Pine Mountain to begin a year of "presenting" as a woman. (As a semiretired investment adviser who oversees the financial affairs of his several clients, he can continue to work at home.) There is, it turns out, a whole protocol for sexual reassignment, safeguards to protect against the disasters of the early years. Often men became women, and women men, expecting miracles, and then, when their whole lives didn't improve dramatically, they became disillusioned, often to the point of suicide. If he-now-she passes muster—i.e., if certain psychological criteria have been met—she'll have genital surgery.

Since June he's been on hormone therapy, under the supervision of an endocrinologist who specializes in transsexuals. Nothing artificial—he's quite insistent on this; he's not going to become some pneumatic babe, a Marilyn Monroe wannabe.

I think about this. "Just one thing," I say (hoping to inject a note of levity, but not entirely joking), "please tell me you'll still be smart at money and computers, and not dumb like . . . well, like a girl? Like me? Or Eleanor or Beth." None of us can go a week without having a computer emergency and appealing to him for assistance.

"I'll still be the same person inside," he reassures me. And as such, something of an exception. According to what he's read and to doctors he's talked with, most transsexuals on hormones change more psychologically than physically, but so far, it seems to be the opposite with him. I'm not ready for details, but I think this is a relief.

He's begun taking instruction in feminine dress and comportment— how to talk the talk and walk the walk—from a professional, a woman in Santa Cruz who specializes in transsexuals. Apparently, there's a whole cottage industry, a surgical-cosmetic complex, geared to the transitioning male. (The females to males, still considered a minority within a minority, have different needs and physical goals.) And then there's electrolysis, which he must undergo every two months, in California, and it's excruciating.

His plans are as precisely coordinated as a military campaign, involving a whole set of changes that must occur overnight. Nothing can be done by increments. Change of dress and hair (a wig at first), as well as name on Social Security card and driver's license—all of these will take place simultaneously and by stealth, so that Chevey will disappear and Ellen, like Athena emerging from the head of Zeus, will go forth fully armed as a woman. She will be legally—if not yet anatomically—a female and, one hopes, a socially convincing one. It's scary, like Kafka's *Metamorphosis* or the transformation when the fairy godmother waves her magic wand. One day he is John Haskell, Eleanor's husband (no shopping for female clothes, no fingernail polish) and the stepfather of her two children; the next day he is a she, Ellen Hampton, a guy-gal in a wig.

And the worst part (other than the fear of failure as a woman) is the facial reconstruction, the surgery with which Chevey has decided to start in order to give himself every advantage. (It goes without saying that these alterations are hugely expensive; luckily, he's always been a saver rather than a spender.) The facial reconstruction, in which the face is hacked up and reassembled, eliminating masculine characteristics, is far more arduous and difficult than genital surgery, and his description is the most convincing evidence of the overwhelming power of the transsexual's urge to change. It will last upwards of ten hours, and after coming out of it, he'll look, in his words, "like someone who's gone eight rounds with Mike Tyson, without gloves." Eleanor, in an act of astonishing generosity, will accompany him for the surgery and bring him home to live with her for a period of recovery. As soon as he, at that point she, is able to take care of herself—drive a car, go to the grocery store—she'll leave and go to Pine Mountain as Ellen.

And then, if the facial surgery succeeds (and what is success?), there's the perilous aftermath. Will she be safe? Transsexuals are particularly susceptible to deadly assault (see the film *Boys Don't Cry*). They're a lightning rod for sexual sadists sniffing out a victim, or for men who feel threatened by the in-your-face sexual confusion they introduce, and Chevey is a particularly tall lightning rod.

"And what about, well, sexual orientation? Will you be... heterosexual or homosexual?"

"It's not about sex," he stresses, "it's about identity."

Nevertheless, he will be heterosexual, a heterosexual female who would like, but doesn't necessarily expect, to meet a man. My brother, almost sixty years old and six feet tall, will be a "woman on the loose." My heart stops. The danger. The grotesqueness. An aging transsexual. Terence Stamp in *The Adventures of Priscilla, Queen of the Desert*, sad, dignified, last chance at love: a sweet, grizzled, elderly mechanic in the outback. Or Dustin Hoffman's desperate frump of an actress in *Tootsie*. What's the best we can hope for? That he'll be more comely than Dame Edna, but not quite as dishy as Jaye Davidson in *The Crying Game*?

Yet there is nothing of the flamboyant gender rebel in Chevey. What makes it unusual is precisely my brother's conservatism: a guy's guy to all appearances, manly, reserved, twice married to wonderful wives, from a city, or from a *section* of that city, where gays are still closeted, the word "feminism" is never heard, and no one has voted Democrat since Harry Truman (which they lived to regret). To be specific, we are talking about Richmond's West End, the very antipode of those meccas of blurred gender San Francisco and the anything-goes subcultures of New York. Simply put, when, in the two most recent presidential elections, Virginia became a swing state for Obama, these Richmonders were not the swingers.

Chevey and I grew up, and he has stayed, in this lovely, sedate, gene-proud Capital of the Confederacy. Or rather, since Richmond has changed tumultuously in the last twenty years, a certain ultra-WASP section of Richmond that has remained quietly but defiantly resistant to time: staid, tasteful, the high-church altar of the Old Dominion's patron saints—Washington, Madison, Jefferson, Clay—with many of its handsome residential areas situated on the James River, that most historic river, now tainted by present-day pollution and its past as a major transportation route for newly arrived African slaves.

The conservatism and tradition of good manners, which I can appreciate more with the passage of time, made our quarter of the world an ideal place in which to grow up: secure; families intact; children given enough freedom but not too much. It was a generally somnolent era that was free of so much of the political and personal turmoil that would roil postsixties America. But this calm surface, this wholesomeness, with all its taboos and secrets, exacted its price in conformity and repression. There was segregation, of course, always present and rarely discussed. Richmond was on the wrong side of history where race was concerned, but I was on the wrong side of Richmond, or would have been if I'd given voice to my mutinous thoughts. I remember having discussions with a friend, the only one I knew to have liberal tendencies, in almost hushed tones. We hated the fact that blacks had to ride at the back of the bus, but an activist I wasn't. My chosen course would be to leave altogether.

Whatever its virtues and defects, Richmond as we know it is not the kind of place that fosters alternate lifestyles or ethnic diversity, much less "gender confusion"! "Don't stand out" is the fundamental axiom of the tribe, the price of belonging, and deviation could mean ostracism. We children all grew up in lockstep, went to the same schools, belonged to the same clubs, learned to dance at cotillion, were confirmed and worshipped in the Episcopal or Presbyterian churches. Moreover, the "good" families would have paid to keep their names *out* of the paper—not just from fear a burglar might strike if news of a trip leaked out, but simply because people like us didn't promote or advertise ourselves. In truth, these families didn't actually go on many trips. They were too content to stay in Richmond. Those Trollope novels where everyone has to be in London for "the season"? Well, in Richmond's West End the season was all year long. And the next and the next. Oh, a trip to Europe was fine once in a while, and Florida in the winter (provided one stayed at one of the resorts colonized by fellow Richmonders), but what place on earth, what people, could compare with Richmond? When the European tour became de rigueur for the teenage set, a friend explained why she had to postpone the pleasure: "If you go to France, you have to go for at least a week, and I'd miss too much in Richmond." The tribe was more important than the individual and the individual took her identity from the tribe.

Don't get me wrong: growing up there was a privilege, and as a child and teenager I loved the place. Indeed, my escape would have been so much easier and less fraught had I loved it less. But Chevey and I had taken the escape route of marriage. I'd left, moved to New York, and, to Mother's dismay, wedded a film critic from Queens, the son of Greek immigrants no less. As the American importer of France's "auteur theory," Andrew Sarris would gain recognition as an important and provocative force in the explosion of sixties cinephilia, but at the time he was just one more idiosyncratic voice on the masthead of an "underground" weekly called the *Village Voice* that no one in Richmond had ever heard of. And through marriage, Chevey had removed himself from the rigidities of haute WASP social circles, had rejected the "place for themselves" that my parents, not native Virginians, had worked so hard to establish. His wives were not (and were not interested in being) "old Richmond," which—it now strikes me—allowed Chevey to keep pretty much to himself.

I was the official family renegade, the turncoat; he the apparently staid and dependable stay-at-home. I'd become a transplanted New Yorker of more-or-less liberal persuasion; Chevey was a moderate, but Richmond was still his city, his people. However little he might participate in their rituals, they shared a certain DNA, were bound together by—if nothing else—an overpowering sense of the importance of discretion. And now . . . ? Transsexuals are everywhere, we're told. Presumably, like the saints in the Episcopal children's hymn, "you can meet them in school, or in lanes, or at sea, in church, or in trains, or in shops, or at tea."

But in Richmond?

Actually, Chevey would be discreet, even about becoming a transsexual, and Richmond would be discreet in its reaction.

On the day he leaves his and Eleanor's house and moves to Pine Mountain, a letter will go out to business acquaintances, close friends, and family, informing them that John Cheves Haskell Jr. has become Ellen Clark Hampton. Why this name? Why choose the name Ellen, so close to his wife's? Because, he tells me, it's the name he called himself in his fantasy life, and the fantasy life is where his soul and spirit lived, took sustenance. And why not keep our last name, Haskell? Because he doesn't want to embarrass the family. Clark is my mother's maiden name, Hampton a family name deriving from our forebear Wade Hampton, the South Carolina Civil War general, U.S. senator, and postwar governor. There is a delicious irony in this, as Chevey, never much interested in family history, has chosen just the name that would chill the blue blood of our relatives who put great stock in genealogy, and many of whose children, male and female, bear the first name Hampton. But Chevey just liked the sound of it; as he began to live more and more as the woman in his head, these were the details in which he wrapped himself, the saving fantasy of who he "really" was and can't now abandon.

Andrew and I are instructed not to breathe a word until the letters go out in early May, some months from now. And then, only moments after he's made his revelation, he says, "You have to promise me one thing." Anything, anything. "You won't write about this." I nod. Unhappy, but what can I say? In a matter of hours, I'll begin to have second thoughts and even come up with a title ("My Brother My Sister"), only half joking, but for now I would agree to anything. An earlier memoir I wrote about Andrew and his near-fatal illness infuriated my mother and distressed Chevey almost as much on her behalf. For the moment, however, writing about it would have to be the furthest thing from my mind.

After Chevey goes home, I continue to rack my memory for early signs, sissy behavior, and find none. Andrew is equally shocked. Eleanor and I call each other every day. She is now my companion in commiseration, in fear. We have long, agonized conversations. She has known for six months about the change but remains equally flabbergasted.

I go to my analyst, who seems nonplussed by the news of my brother. No, that's not quite right. I go to my analyst and begin by burying the lead. "I want to come less often." He nods. Then I say, "My brother is going to become a woman." His jaw doesn't drop, but his eyebrows rise several millimeters—the shrink equivalent. "Why didn't you tell me that first?" he asks.

The wish to cut back on my number of weekly appointments has been preying on my mind for some time. I haven't mentioned it—I was afraid of "hurting his feelings" (an "issue" that I managed to avoid discussing for seven years)—and here was an opportunity to get it out of the way in a hurry.

Andrew goes to his therapist, with whom he has a more conversational relationship and who expresses real surprise. "Why would he do it now," he asks, "at an age when women are losing their desirability?" Apparently, neither therapist has had any experience, direct or otherwise, with transsexuals.

"Maybe he'll change his mind," Eleanor and I say more than once, a desperate hope. She, too, is seeing a therapist because, she says, "there's so much I can't discuss with anybody. He doesn't give me any ideas about how to move forward, just gives me the free space to vent, and I mostly sit there and bawl."

And we worry. What's going to happen to him living alone in the mountains? Why won't he join a support group, meet other transsexuals? I ask him. He says he's "not one of them." (We can't call him "she" yet, even when projecting into the future.) Eleanor's lawyer knew someone, a male-to-female transsexual, and offered to introduce them—she might at least provide information—but Chevey didn't want to.

Andrew and I make jokes. About . . . Chevey's refusal to join a support group or meet others in the same situation. Andrew says, "That's all we need, an uptight transsexual."

Eleanor and I also make jokes to cover our apprehension, our fears for him and for ourselves (the snickers and eyeball-rolling). About what s/he's going to look like, sound like. Barbara, Eleanor's daughter, says her mother should have surgery and become a man and they could stay married. Chevey did suggest that, as Virginia law permitted it, they might stay married, but Eleanor vetoed that, saying it wouldn't work for either of them.

CHAPTER TWO

Flesh and Blood

And now again obscurity descends, and would indeed that it were deeper! . . . But let other pens treat of sex and sexuality; we quit such odious subjects as soon as we can.

—Virginia Woolf, *Orlando*

*W*ould indeed that it were all a dream. Or a jeu d'esprit, like the Virginia Woolf novel *Orlando*, about a time-travelling, gender-morphing acrobat, whose overnight change is both "painless and complete." If only we could draw a veil of obscurity over the less poetic reality. But in the all-too-literal real world, my brother is to become my sister. And in the decidedly unlyrical vocabulary of such things, he is transgender (genus) and transsexual (species), making a complete "transition," which includes the rearrangement of those crude body parts that Virginia Woolf airily transcended.

No, it isn't illness or death, and thank heaven for that.

But the upside of illness and death is that there are guidelines for how to behave, even what to feel. Books and movies and even life itself have given us a repertory of words and gestures appropriate to major crises and events. With death there's a ritual framework, the formalities of bereavement, according to which friends and relatives gather round and offer concern and support. Like a mild anesthetic, it doesn't obliterate the pain but takes the edge off, lifts you out of your solitary self. Here, we're in uncharted seas. I'm not allowed to summon friends, even if I wanted to (and I don't, not now). And what is an adversity for me is (however perilous) a liberation for my brother. I suppose there is, tucked into every strong response, a hidden opposite: mixed with the intense grief over a loved one's death is the shadow of relief, the escape from emotional dependency; the happiness of the marital vows is undercut by the isolation of "forsaking all others"; the whole world of conventional pain and pleasure disappears in the madness of *l'amour fou*; and the act of sex shudders with the *petit mort* of mortality foretold. But with my brother, the predominant note is "mixed feelings." What to do with "gender reassignment"? There is no precedent for my brother's decision, hence no way to orchestrate my confusion. How can you grieve when the person you love is brimful of hope for the future? Where does it fit into the taxonomy of life crises when one person's liberation is another's loss?

I see it as a changing of identities, like someone on the lam, or going into the witness protection program. He sees it, quite the reverse, as someone who's been living as a fake, who's already done time in the witness protection program and can finally come clean, walk out the door, and face the light of day as his, or rather her, true self. A more extreme version, perhaps, of other kinds of medical miracles—for example, someone who's suffered from schizophrenia or bipolar disorder or lifelong depression and is finally given an effective drug and comes out of the fog into something like normalcy. Or the clarity of vision that can come after cataract surgery. Or "cosmetic" surgery not for vanity or youth but to remove scars or a birth defect.

Another thought, selfish but overwhelming: suppose something happens to Andrew! This fear is never far from my mind. My husband is extremely infirm, an imbalance of the legs not just from old age (he is approaching eighty) but from nerve damage sustained during a terrifying, near-fatal illness in 1984. He walks unsteadily with a cane, is hard of hearing. He looks and feels old. He is still teaching, but the incredible extemporaneous lectures, the broad range of associations, are becoming a thing of the past as his thinking and speaking slow down.

I love Andrew so, I think to myself, and I don't know how I'll live without him, but if he dies, the one person I'll want first—have always assumed will be there to get me through it all, logistically and emotionally—is my brother. But now he'll be—Ellen. Could I face a memorial service for Andrew with everyone gawking at my "sister"? Could I face friends coming over, having to make introductions? In such an emergency, who would I lean on? My anxiety on this score is isolating and shameful, but it turns out Eleanor is also suffering along these lines. Her mother, ailing and at home with caregivers, will probably die in the next year or so. Chevey is very close to Mrs. W, almost a surrogate son. But, unable to confess, Eleanor has simply told her mother they've broken up (shock enough!). Mrs. W is never to know of Ellen, and Ellen won't be welcome at the funeral. Eleanor will give out the same story to her sister and friends at church, but she feels uncomfortable skirting the truth. . . . Suppose they ask questions?

I call a friend, the psychoanalyst Ethel Person, the one human being I've been granted permission by Chevey to talk to. Ethel is known for her referrals—for expertly pairing patients with analysts (she gave me mine back in 1987)—but, more important, she's written about transsexuals and has made them something of a subspecialty in her practice. She takes the news in stride. "Transsexuals are the best, the kindest people I know," she says, "maybe because they have to learn compassion the hard way."

I tell her that Chevey—or John, as Eleanor calls him—was hurt by Eleanor's refusal to bring her mother in on the secret. "He longs for validation," Ethel says, and spoke of transsexualism as being "a passion of the soul." If only I knew what that meant.

I try to get hold of myself, embrace the positive spin. After all, I am losing a brother not to mortality but to sisterhood. And he is gaining his identity, his "authenticity," his soul. My instinct—for myself, for Eleanor, for everyone including him—is to think of it as a catastrophe. Not just for our lives, but for his: how will he, when she, live alone up there on the mountain? Will she be persecuted, shunned, or even in danger? But he wants it too much for me to think in purely negative terms.

When we talk on the phone I can hear the excitement in Chevey's voice. I know the anxiety is there, but he's buoyed by the anticipation of moving forward. I ask about his activities and preparations.

"The dilemma was always that on a particular day not far off I'd become Ellen, but until that time, I had to be Chevey living with Eleanor. As Chevey I can't go around and try on women's clothes, yet once I become Ellen I have to have a wardrobe."

Through the recommendation of his endocrinologist, he found Lisa, a partner in a trendy local salon. He told her his problem (she was gay, as it turned out, and they became friends), and she suggested a woman in Charlottesville who was a clothing designer and had a little shop there.

That was how Chevey found Janice, and the two of them worked out a plan. She measured him and assessed his needs, and when he visited her every week or so, she would have a variety of outfits from different stores assembled for him. Sneaking into a back room, he would try them on, buying one or two and discarding the rest, so that over the course of several months, he gradually accumulated a basic wardrobe—as well as "lots of excellent advice."

"Some of it I already knew from my years of observing women, studying how they looked and walked, but certain things I didn't know, the finer points, like does the shirttail look right in or out, how to tie a sash, things that as a guy you just wouldn't have any way of knowing.

"It was expensive, because I had to pay her and buy the clothes, too. And driving to Charlottesville so often was inconvenient, but I didn't want to do it in Richmond; I was trying not to embarrass Eleanor. So Janice was a real lifesaver."

That night I dream that my brother is a beautiful girl, with blond hair and young skin. I wake up thinking, "I wish!" On the other hand, if the dream does come true, if Ellen is young and beautiful, will I be jealous? He's younger than I am, and has always looked extremely young for his age.

I am happy he's in such good hands, has done all this to prepare himself. And yet, I'm ashamed to admit, it makes me cringe. I begin collecting transgender stories, just in case Chevey's ban against writing is lifted, and I look at these stories and say, "Why must they?" As I clip and file, I also avert my eyes, put off reading. Some religious fundamentalist in me arises, demanding, Can't they just accept the bodies God gave them? Even as I am coming to understand a little of the nature of the urge, how overpowering it is, how little a *choice*—I want to keep my brother. It's fine, even a bit titillating, for other people's children or siblings or parents or friends to change sex, but this is too close to home. I long, atavistically, for the manly ideal, the "oak tree" male.

There is also resentment: who does he, or rather *she*, think she is? Claiming womanhood without having had to go through the trials and travails (menopause, childbirth, general and especially body insecurity). Trying to have it both ways. (Of course, trying to pass as a woman at sixty, she can hardly be said to have escaped body insecurity!) Most of all, why would a man give up his perks, not to mention the Big Kahuna, to become a woman at precisely the age when women are becoming invisible crones? And the reassessment: How will this recast our childhood? How will it undermine my images of family? Will memories have to be altered to accommodate the brother—or should I say "sister"—I never knew?

And then, of course—how can one avoid it—what will people think? (Thank God Mother is dead.) I know, it's happening more and more often; soon it will be common enough that it will be accepted, especially by the younger generation. *But I'm not a member of the younger generation.*

In a memorable *New Yorker* article (1997) on Teena Brandon, a.k.a. Brandon Teena, "The Humboldt Murders," John Gregory Dunne speculates as to what an earlier and even more famous transgressive woman of the West, Willa Cather, would have made of the gender-crossing Teena. Cather loved women and created in her tomboy Antonia a heroine very like the poor rural androgyne whose murder became the subject of the Hilary Swank film *Boys Don't Cry.* "One can assume," Dunne writes, "that Cather would have regarded her [Teena's] obsession with gender and its discontents as self-indulgent, and her gender confusion as an excuse to abdicate personal responsibility."

Cather may have shared geography with Brandon Teena but the writer had the advantage of a large, close-knit family and an old-fashioned sense of decorum that went with it. She would have had no experience of Teena's knockabout life of abuse and poverty. But surely that exasperation with "self-indulgence" rings a chord among those of us who came to adulthood before the efflorescence of gender identity politics, with each minority's claims of persecution and prejudice, clamors for recognition, and determination to set matters aright whatever the cost. That I'm on both sides of the divide—part traditionalist, part liberationist—doesn't make the whole thing any easier. Even the feminist that I am, by definition a supporter of minority rights, is staggered by the speed of change and the shape those rights have taken. The struggle for women's equality seems downright quaint, a settled issue, compared to such recent commonplaces as single parents, gay marriage, gay parents, test-tube babies, sperm donors, and egg surrogates.

Why should I be shocked? Back in 2001, I wrote an essay for the *New York Times* Arts & Leisure section ("In the Land of Self-Invention, You Can Always Start Over") about the Second Chance narrative as "a phenomenon that has always existed but that has somehow taken on greater urgency and inventiveness in our age of long lives and multiple choices." In the films covered by the article, "a beleaguered protagonist has the opportunity, either through outside intervention or inner transformation, to do it over or better." I attributed the proliferation of such stories to the fact that "we are seduced daily by visions of other places and possibilities, thereby living parallel lives in our heads . . . a function of rising divorce rates, feminism's multiple-choice agenda, and the life-span statistics on the actuarial tables. We have more time to evolve, change, rewind."

I don't think I had sex change in mind, nor could I ever be quite as cavalier as I sounded.

My brother and I grew up in a world that was still late Victorian in its attitudes toward sex and everything else. There were euphemisms for body parts and most of their functions; family secrets were best kept that way. In most ways, the South was behind the rest of the country—industrially, economically, politically, racially, even "sexually." But socially was a different matter. We socialized early, were precocious imbibers, but with our elders as mentors, so that we would learn how to "hold our liquor" and conduct ourselves in public. At the age of thirteen my classmates and I, wearing party dresses and gloves, went to cotillion every other Saturday night. The stationing of the boys on one side of the dance floor and the girls on the other, observed by strategically placed chaperones, was an apt configuration of the divide between the sexes. The boys asked or were nudged into asking the girls to dance, never the other way around, and the taller girls—I speak from stinging memories of humiliation—were more likely to be wallflowers . . . an early lesson in rejection and preparation for many to come. These Saturday nights were training sessions, the prelims in the stage-by-stage initiation into the privileges and penalties of the tribe. Next was debutante year, the final induction ceremony before the summum bonum of matrimony. We painted ourselves for the first time, drank firewater, and danced around our elite Holy Wasp campfire sites.

No less socially preordained than I, Chevey came along five and a half years later, mastering the lessons in gentlemanly behavior. He would have to walk across the ballroom and lead a girl onto the floor when perhaps he wished to be the one in the taffeta dress, the one invited to dance. These rites were like the swaddling blankets in the crib, intended to ease the transit from the enclosure of the womb—keeping us safe and secure but unable to move freely.

I ask him on the phone if he has memories of cotillion. He recalls going for three of the customary four years, before being sent off to boarding school.

"And yes, I always felt I could be on the other side. I vividly remember an evening when, in some sort of contest, three or four boys dressed as girls, one in a woman's one-piece bathing suit! To me it was excruciating, because I was always trying to suppress the urge and then something like this would bring it up."

"And naturally you didn't volunteer to be one of the cross-dressers?"

"God, no. I would have been terrified to do something like that—afraid I would be too convincing. I was always going to the opposite extreme."

Another cotillion memory: they always had car pools, one for girls, one for boys. We were living in the country so it was a good long ride. One year he simply decided to switch to the girls' group. At the time, he didn't make much of it, just thought—correctly, as it turned out—that it would be more fun.

Thinking of this old-world mind-set as against the "do your own gender thing" attitude of so many young people, I wonder if Chevey (as I shall think of him until he becomes Ellen) doesn't fall between two camps: on one side, the older generation (to which he belongs chronologically), so many of whom feel an impatience bordering on aversion to "transgender," along with an inability to even remotely understand it, and on the other side, the young people of liberal persuasion who think it's no big deal—indeed, who wonder, why change sex at all? Why not live according to how you feel at the moment? It's the "person," not the sex, that matters.

I came up against this while teaching in the graduate writing program at an Eastern college famous as the last outpost of sixties-style hippiedom, and a virtual laboratory in gender experimentation. Here, gender was being constructed and deconstructed daily, and in ways that were more than theoretical. A friend was teaching in the same department and realized one of her students was "in transition," but she didn't know—and the student hadn't disclosed—which sex s/he was departing from and which joining. She decided to send an e-mail asking if the student had a preferred pronoun, and was relieved when the student wrote back "he."

My own students were similarly resistant to "labels" like male and female, and my firsthand introduction to the New Democrats of Gender came when a student read a piece that took place in a beauty salon. There were two characters, the beautician and the client, but as to whether they were male or female there was no clue, and none emerged as the story unfolded. Finally I stopped her and said we had to know what sex they were. Since everyone considered me a fogey, she glanced at her classmates for support, but this time they nodded in agreement with me. Even these believers in "gender fluidity," who would never use the term "actress," felt we needed the specifics.

According to the doctrine of inclusiveness and everyone-must-be-invited-to-the-birthday-party, any label or category cuts off avenues of self-invention or hybrid selves. This was a subtheme of the postcolonial multicultural ideal, like the movement toward rejecting those forms requiring people to identify themselves as "White," "Black," "Hispanic," or even "Other," in favor of a response like "All of the above" or "Some combination thereof." What is Obama but a mixed-race president who decided early on to be identified not as "All of the above" but as black. For me there's a world of difference between the *idea* of multiple selves and the real-life drama by which a man gives up his penis for a vagina and a woman loses her brother of nearly sixty years.

Famished for information, and following my tendency to intellectualize unmanageable problems by turning to books, I devour both memoirs and scientific studies on the subject, and find examples of other transsexuals, hoping for comfort and enlightenment. I desire knowledge, the more the better. Perhaps understanding—quite a different thing—will come later. Possibly I shall find a psychoanalytic explanation, a category for my brother, in Robert Stoller's *Sex and Gender: The Transsexual Experiment* or Mildred Brown and Chloe Ann Rounsley's *True Selves*. See where he fits in historically in Susan

Stryker's *Transgender History*. And a view from inside in Jan Morris's *Conundrum*, a memoir which I read and admired when it first came out, and Jennifer Finney Boylan's *She's Not There*, which Chevey offered as a hostess-cum-initiation present on his announcement visit. He'd given instructional copies to Beth and Eleanor as well. Transsexuals are lucky to have as literary ambassadresses two such wise and witty self-appraisers. Jan was James Morris, Oxford-Sandhurst graduate, officer in the Queen's Royal Lancers, distinguished journalist and travel writer. The vocation fits: the appetite for far-flung continents and cultures and the ability to slip into other people's skins may have come naturally to this childhood wanderer and future gender-émigré with his sense of uprootedness, of being "a creature of wisp or spindrift." Morris was fortunate in being born into a country, a class, a family where eccentricity is indulged, and to have come into an uncertain manhood at Oxford, a place that, as she sees it, is hospitable to "misfits," since there was no normative "fit" from which to deviate.

As an adult prior to the transition, s/he may have encountered terrors that go with living in a gender no-man's-land, surely more than are present in her book, which resolutely avoids anger and self-pity, but no one, it strikes me, appears to have been more at ease straddling the sexes. The officer (confident, authoritative) and the gentlewoman (flexible, self-deprecating) adapt, even thrive, in ambiguous situations. At the security check at Kennedy Airport, Morris, now in midtransition, simply awaits a signal—a "madam" or a "sir"—to guide her into the appropriate frisking queue. As a world traveller who sees beyond Western-style binaries, she herself might be one of those gods or shamans of myth she cites, a fusion figure with supernatural powers who represents and celebrates the complementarity of the sexes.

Fate has been similarly kind to Jennifer Finney Boylan. James Boylan, professor of writing at Colby, wrote picaresque comic novels in a John Irving vein (though with less castration anxiety!), was married with two children, and watched sports on television with his best friend, the novelist Richard Russo. As Jenny, she continues to teach but has exchanged the novelist's polyphonic voice for that of the memoirist and essayist, often appearing on *Oprah* and writing smart op-ed pieces for the *New York Times*, many on transgender matters.

It's easy to see why Chevey loves Boylan's account of his (her?) transition: it is not only funny but triumphalist, as opposed to the more troubled life of Renée Richards, not just as a tennis player but as the parent of a deeply unhappy son. Like Morris, Boylan manages to keep her family—wife and children—together. Both describe early stirrings in similar terms. Boylan's first sense of living the wrong life came when as a little boy he was watching his mother iron his father's shirts. Someday, his mother tells him, he will wear shirts like this, and James feels an instantaneous recoil. Like Chevey, neither of these authors, as children or teenagers, could describe a "condition." They simply felt an indefinable falseness. Morris asserts it had nothing to do with a desire to be *feminine*. Rather, "it had everything to do with being *female*."

"To me," she writes, "gender is not physical at all, but is altogether insubstantial. It is soul, perhaps, it is talent, it is taste, it is environment, it is how one feels, it is light and shade, it is inner music. . . . It is the essentialness of oneself, the psyche, the fragment of unity. Male and female are sex, masculine and feminine are gender, and though the conceptions obviously overlap, they are far from synonymous."

Chevey read and admired *Conundrum,* but it's Boylan's *She's Not There* that had a life-altering effect.

"When I read it," he tells me, "and saw the things she would think, they were exactly the things that I had thought time and again. I had found myself thinking the same phrases, trying to understand, and here she had felt and expressed them, practically word for word. I could relate to her personally in a way I couldn't to Christine Jorgensen or Renée Richards. I saw interviews with them that didn't interest me, but Jenny was a revelation. And the weirdest part of all was that when she would quote things that her wife, Grace, had said, I would sit there dumbfounded, thinking that it was almost verbatim what Eleanor had said three weeks ago. And I thought, *Wow, what is going on here?* There is a whole lot more going on than just an emotional state. Because an emotional state wouldn't have people in different parts of the country thinking and feeling the same words."

Fascinated as I am, these optimistic memoirs don't allow room for my own stupefaction, resentment, shock—on Eleanor's behalf as well as my own—feelings I imagine most close relatives must experience at one time or another. Was Morris's wife really as comfortable as Jan indicates? Ditto Boylan's? Russo we know was blindsided, and critical—he writes a very funny and poignant epilogue that hits home more than Boylan's upbeat accounts. He couldn't believe it wasn't a "choice." And what about the failures? The transsexuals who were disappointed, even devastated, whose lives didn't turn out better? Presumably, failures don't write memoirs.

I suppose I am still in stage one or two of grief: Denial and Anger. Not ready for Acceptance. As Chevey has embarked on a leap into the unknown, I need to give him my love and support, but also to find my own way to wherever I'm destined to go with this. So far I seem to be alone.

It is early 2006, and I pay a visit to Ethel before going to a women writers' dinner at Martha's, a gathering I dread and now wish I could skip altogether. At these friendly gossiping-and-venting sessions, we may discuss politics or cultural events, but that's only the warm-up for the main course: ourselves and our writing dilemmas. We go around the room, each woman describing her current vexations, professional and personal: difficulties with publishers (she can't find one), editors (they don't call back), personal-memoir dilemmas, writing blocks, and significant others, whereupon the rest chime in with advice, parallel problems, and other forms of reassurance or counsel. Throughout my life, I've found enormous strength and consolation in the company of women. As a teenager I wouldn't have survived my father's illness and death without school and schoolmates; during my recent and ongoing anxieties regarding Andrew, friendships have been a major sustenance. But in my present predicament, these crucial outlets—friends and writing—are closed off to me as a source of comfort, as is the balm that might come simply by the airing of my secret. When I tell Ethel that my main concern is how and when to tell people, she replies, "You don't have to tell." Which is meant to reassure me but is no reassurance at all. Perhaps it's partly that I want to control the news, can't bear the idea of it leaking out and people discussing it behind my back, but it has more to do with my nature: I would rather shout it from the rooftops than retreat into shameful isolation in a way that only further stigmatizes the condition it's meant to protect.

Ethel adds ominously: "What people think and what they say are two different things."

Before trying to embrace this new reality, I can't help playing devil's advocate, taking a look at the loss and hurt involved, even the desire to look away—another form of ostracism. Transsexual autobiographers— Morris, Boylan, Christine Jorgensen, Renée Richards, Deirdre McCloskey—are a remarkably smart and sympathetic lot. Their memoirs range from good to excellent, all brave, sometimes funny, describing and embracing their condition and making an overt or implicit plea for tolerance. But what about those of us left to pick up the pieces? While I'm certainly for tolerance, I can also sympathize with those struck dumb, who simply can't get their minds around why an apparently normal and successful person would want to switch sexes in middle age, or later. Is gender, as Boylan says, really as "malleable as sand"? And my brother's life has been so honest and honorable. Chevey has been not just beyond reproach but deeply loved and appreciated! How unlikely a candidate he seemed, how far from the stereotype we imagine. But I have to ask: how unlikely is he? He's a far cry from those flamboyant and campy images from popular culture, but do we have an image of the transsexual as pathological or cutting edge or flaky just because, in a hostile environment, those who've had the temerity to go through with it tend to be people already closer to the margins, further from the mainstream, to begin with?

It's precisely the spectacle of "normal" people changing sex that brings into the open the real fear: not difference but sameness. The degree to which there is already so dangerously much of the female in the male and vice versa.

The feminist theoretician Judith Butler, leading exponent of the idea of "performativity" and of gender as a socially constructed role, advances the notion of mourning for the sex one isn't. There is a kind of unconscious grief, a yearning for what we have lost or never had. The ambiguity of sex begins early on. Weeks into human life, the fetus is chromosomally female, XX, before (if the fetus is a male) the Y chromosome replaces one of the Xs and we go our separate ways—or not so separate, for as Freud maintained, we all begin as bisexuals. And we may cling to our respective gender teams all the more anxiously because becoming a man or a woman is never smooth sailing.

In the course of the Oedipus complex, the boy must tear himself away from the powerful mother of the nursery, become a man precisely to escape *femaleness*. But that escape is never final; masculinity must be on constant guard against the incursion of the feminine. As most observers will tell you, preschoolers are far more rigid in enforcing sexual stereotypes than are adults.

What we used to call sex and now, faute de mieux, call "gender" is fundamental, our first identity, our last certitude. "Deeper down than we are rich and poor, black and white," wrote Theodore Roszak, "we are he and she. This is the last ditch of our socially prescribed identity . . . the one line of our psychic defense we dare not surrender." No wonder the panic that arises at the prospect of someone breaching that divide finds expression (or protection) in all sorts of adverse reactions: incredulity, hostility, disapproval, anger.

Not only popular culture but most religions exalt the male over the female, a preference explicitly rendered in the Orthodox Jewish prayer "Blessed are you, Lord, our God, ruler of the universe, who has not created me a woman." And what about the manic obsession with the male member in recent stand-up comedy: could it spring from a fear that the penis isn't quite the supreme commander it once was?

For all my proud stance as a diversity-championing New Yorker, a let-many-flowers-bloom feminist/liberal, this seemed to have nothing to do with tolerance and was beyond understanding. You don't have to be a redneck bigot in the Borat mold to feel the ground is shifting too quickly.

The one person who seems completely at peace with the transition, even happy it will finally take place, is Beth, Chevey's first wife. She found out about Chevey's longing and problem—when he himself had found the words for it—in 1976, eight years into their marriage. Somehow she managed her grief and sorrow, and became his ally and fellow traveller into this unknown world. She is happily remarried; she is also a militant liberal. Unlike Eleanor and me, she simply can't understand why others can't get with the program.

"There is so much prejudice," she says with exasperation when we talk on the phone. "Why can't people just accept different norms for different people!"

"But doesn't this seem like one outrage, one plea for tolerance, too many?" I'm thinking the body politic is patting itself on the back for having come to terms with homosexuality, even homosexual marriage, and now they're being asked to accept this phenomenon that in most people's eyes is far more freakish, more of an outrage against nature.

Instead of getting angry at Chevey, I displace my exasperation onto all other transsexuals. He's genuine, they're phonies. All the arguments I use in his favor are suddenly out the window when it comes to the others. If I can't reject *him*, I can them. My anger takes the form of: they are *choosing* this, why can't they choose *not* to do it! I realize it's not just the confusion it introduces about gender, and our faith in a "natural" sexual identity. Worse, possibly, is the challenge it poses to our faith in free will: hence our insistence on the word "choice."

Someone tells me about a documentary on the Discovery Channel about people with a certain type of obsessional disorder in which the afflicted believe a body part doesn't belong to them, and want nothing more than to get rid of it. As a transsexual wants to be relieved of his penis, a man in the film wants to get rid of an offending leg. After hours of therapy, and knowing full well it's irrational, he plunges his leg into a freezing solution, contracts gangrene, and, after having his leg amputated, feels blissful relief. In a similar vein, the movie *Quid Pro Quo* (2008) features an eerily fascinating subculture of able-bodied men and women who fantasize and play at being disabled, among them a curator, played by the always adventurous Vera Farmiga, who wants passionately to be wheelchair-bound. What these psychic phenomena share is an inexplicable desire to become what the world sees as less rather than more, maimed rather than whole. Whatever the psychological underpinnings, the fantasy is for them the reality. Their mental image of their deformed selves so dominates their existence that only by bringing their bodies into line with that image can they achieve a sense of peace and "normalcy."

When we talk of fantasy here, we mean a force far more all-encompassing than the everyday notion of "daydream" or conscious wish. Psychoanalysts have given us this modern (Freudian) definition of fantasy as a governing but unconscious principle of our lives, a shaper of personality that rumbles along like a powerful underground train, more often than not taking us in directions that have little to do with what we think we want. Freud and Proust anticipated current discoveries in neuroscience, Freud with his exploration of the unconscious and the play of primitive and unacknowledged superstitions, Proust with his insights into the foreignness of one's mind and behavior to one's "self." Now scores of books on neuroscience—scholarly, popular, and in between—examine the exploding field of brain chemistry and our habits of misremembering, and remind us that far from being the captains of our souls, not to mention our fates, we are more like galley slaves, madly rowing as our wayward vessel navigates stormy seas into which murky and unknowable desires have plunged us. Rooted in preverbal experience and the potent undercurrents of family, these propulsive forces of desire, rage, inhibition, and guilt affect the jobs we take (or don't take, or fail at), the people we choose (or reject), our moods and memories. We're constantly reminded of how often we act in ways contrary to our self-interest, or remember only what fits a chosen (or unconscious) scenario. Over and over again, we reenact patterns of behavior and make perverse choices—older men, triangles, neediest cases, wounded or crazy or destructive partners—which fly in the face of reason and which we are "helpless" to correct, and so which are hardly "choices" at all.

These include, but aren't restricted to, sexual fantasies dating from childhood, which the psychoanalyst and writer Robert Stoller did so much to illuminate. A disciple of Freud and pioneering sex-role specialist (he developed the concept of "core gender identity"), Stoller wrote in books like *Perversion* (1975) about the presence of guilt, revenge, and aggression as triggers for pleasure and pain while simultaneously de-pathologizing these feelings and behaviors. He and Dr. Harry Benjamin, known as the "grandfather of transsexuals," were in the forefront of attempts to describe and understand the transsexual. Benjamin, an émigré from Berlin who came to work with Kinsey, developed the Benjamin Standards of Care, which are still in use. The two disagreed, however, as to the origin of transsexualism: Benjamin believed it occurred in utero, while Stoller, at least initially, saw the child as "gender neutral at birth," and stressed the mother's influence. "The transsexual boy," writes Stoller, "begins to show his extreme femininity by age two to three, though the first signs may appear as early as age one."

Since Stoller's work in the sixties and early seventies, his theory has been modified (including, in later years, by Stoller himself) to accommodate wider scientific and psychoanalytic research, placing greater emphasis on genetic or prenatal occurrences, in addition to information yielded by a broader spectrum of transgender types. All of which (bad news to lovers of clarity) makes the condition more mystifying than ever.

CHAPTER THREE

My Brother Kisses His Elbow

Girlboys may nothing more than boygirls need.

—e. e. cummings

"*W*hen did the desire to be female first occur?" I ask Chevey. We are talking on the phone in March of 2006. He has come home from an extremely painful bout of electrolysis on the West Coast and will go to San Francisco in April for the facial feminization surgery.

"I've thought about that question many times. It was at Ashley, when we lived in the country. I distinctly remember going up into your room, which was along the hall and up the steps in the old part of the house, and trying on your clothes when no one was around. I've since tried to go back and figure out how old I was at that time, but I don't have a frame of reference. I guess about six or seven years old. We lived there till I was ten. So that's all I have to go by.

"I do remember times when Mother would say things, not realizing what she was saying. Like one time she mentioned this silly thing, how if you could kiss your elbow it would turn you into a girl. And though on the surface I ignored it, inside I jumped. I know it was idiotic but I must have just about broken my arms a couple of times after that, trying to hold my arm in a door, to see if you could get to your elbow. But, of course, you can't.

"I didn't have, we didn't have, the concept of 'transsexual.'

"It probably wasn't long after I started dressing up that Christine

Jorgensen hit the news. [This would have been 1953, when Chevey was seven.] I happened to be in the room when Mother and Daddy were talking about the news. Most dismissed it. It was a once-in-a-lifetime thing; she was seen as a freak, not as big a deal as Renée Richards was years later. But I must have at least known I didn't want to get caught dressing up; I had the concept of 'sissy.' "

In fact, Christine Jorgensen (1927–1989), the Brooklyn-born professional photographer and ex-G.I. who went to Denmark for surgery in 1952, was not the first but the most world-renowned transsexual. In around 1930 or '31, there were two in Germany, the most famous of whom was a Danish painter named Lili Elbe (né Einar Wegener). Her tragic story (recorded in the book *Man into Woman*) involved a series of experimental surgeries, including the implantation of ovaries, and after only a year, she died. But it was Jorgensen who entered the public spotlight and became a catalyst for other would-be transsexuals, many of whom went to Europe for surgery. She also became a patient of Dr. Harry Benjamin, the German endocrinologist turned sex researcher.

"When I look back," Chevey continues, "I'm surprised and amazed at how my life and my very, very slow transition to being female almost coincide with society's realization of transsexualism—I won't say getting used to it, but just hearing about it more and more. It's actually an incredible leap from the dark ages of the fifties and sixties to the present-day explosion of stories in the papers and on television.

"It was Renée Richards who really turned my life upside down. Christine Jorgensen seemed remote—we wondered if this was truth or fiction. But when Renée Richards appeared on magazine covers in 1976, playing women's tennis, and we learned that she had been an ophthalmologist named Richard Raskind . . . well, that just blew the lid off. Before, I think my feelings of being a boy were stronger than of being a girl, simply because that's all there was."

I agree. There has to be a possibility, an example, even a descriptive language, before such vague feelings and disturbances can coalesce into a concrete "something," a condition, a visual image, a real-life possibility.

The scandal caused by this pivotal event may be hard to remember now. Born in 1933, educated at Harvard, an enlistee in the Navy, ranked male tennis player, this handsome, even beautiful, man became a woman at age forty-one. When she tried to play professional tennis as a woman, she was ostracized by her fellow players, rejected by the crowds, and lampooned in the media—Bob Hope joked with Johnny Carson on *The Tonight Show* that she was her own "mixed doubles team."

Nevertheless, for people like my brother, it was as if lightning had struck, illuminating a path but unleashing a storm of agonies as well.

"When that happened, it all came to the surface. I acknowledged to myself my yearning to be female and told Beth, and that caused my castle walls to crumble. Up to then, I hadn't spent a lot of energy thinking about it, because it simply wasn't in the realm of possibility. Now it seemed there were others out there, and information, and doctors. It was still experimental, of course, but there were doctors who did this!

"I keep repeating this point, but you can't imagine what it was like back then, and why Renée Richards was like a bomb going off. At the time, homosexuality was still in the closet; admitting it would destroy your life. I remember a movie [*Advise and Consent*, 1962], based on a book, about a congressman who commits suicide rather than be exposed as a homosexual."

Yes, the world has changed, at least theoretically. The argument against gender-specificity advanced by my students is gaining currency. Shifting shapes and, in academic-speak, the problematizing of identity represent a retreat from the presumed rigidity of traditional norms: the dominant male and supine female who define each other by their differences. Cutting-edge gender provocateurs like Camille Paglia and Marjorie Garber speak of "the pitfalls of gender assignment" and of our fetishizing gender. The psychoanalyst and author Ken Corbett, in his illuminating *Boyhoods*, actually argues that the terms "male" and "female" have outlived their usefulness as designators of gender identity, as have the prescriptive norms tucked within them. Judith Halberstam, celebrator of butch females in her book *Female Masculinity*, speaks of a "post-gender world." The gender-studies expert Anne Fausto-Sterling (*Myths of Gender: Biological Theories About Women and Men*; "The Five Sexes: Why Male and Female Are Not Enough") has mounted an extensive and scholarly challenge to the rigid division of male and female in Western culture, citing examples of hermaphrodites and other variations in the organization of gender that she insists must be seen as a spectrum.

Even in my cloistered childhood, hints as to the porousness of the sexes turned up in some of the scuzzier forms of entertainment. As a teenager, I went each year to the State Fair with my friends and eagerly sought out the "Half Man, Half Woman" exhibition. With a mixture of horror and giddy fascination, we would place ourselves on the children's side of a curtain that divided us from the adults, who were apparently exposed to the naked body of the hermaphrodite (if that's what "it" was) while we were shown only the upper half. Who knows how we absorbed the implications of this, but certainly the image was hard to erase.

If male and female, masculine and feminine, have become unreliable opposites, transgender has become even more of a blur. And where there were once no words for it, now they proliferate with a vengeance. "Transgender" is, itself, a term whose parts are constantly shifting and overlapping.

The simple taxonomy of TGs-meet-yokels road movies, such as *To Wong Foo, Thanks for Everything! Julie Newmar* and *The Adventures of Priscilla, Queen of the Desert*, seems almost quaint. *To Wong Foo*, which came out in 1995, features Wesley Snipes and Patrick Swayze as prizewinning drag queens and John Leguizamo as the teary wannabe for whom Snipes lays it out: "When a straight man puts on a dress and gets his sexual kicks, he's a transvestite. When a man is a woman trapped in a man's body and has a little operation, he is a transsexual. When a gay man has way too much fashion sense for one gender, he is a drag queen. When a tired little Latin boy puts on a dress, he is simply a boy in a dress."

If only it were so simple.

There are many and ever-changing variants in the ever-blossoming field of "gender nonconformity," from biological aberrations like hermaphroditism (a child born with both sets of genitals) to performance celebrations (drag and female impersonators), all of which challenge the feminine-masculine polarity around which we organize our self-image.

Along the transgender spectrum, female-to-male transsexuals have probably been underrecorded (the one-in-five statistic has recently been adjusted to almost equal). For one thing, it's so much easier for a woman to dress, even act, like a man and pass under the radar than it is for a man to cross-dress without raising eyebrows. For another, the surgery is unsatisfactory (the penis being so much more difficult to create than the vagina). Moreover, female-to-males tend to keep a low profile, withdrawing from the limelight that their counterparts actively seek. The club of "difference," LGBT, now includes "I" for intersex, a coinage as yet without a definition. The gender rebels constantly invent their own lingo (like "genderqueer"—synonymous with "androgynous"), rejecting the medical vocabulary that wafts sulfurically from the laboratory and stigmatizes "disorder" with terms like "sexual dysphoria."

One of the main distinctions and the most important one for our purposes is the difference between *transvestism* and *transsexualism*.

A *transvestite*, or cross-dresser, is a man, most often heterosexual, who occasionally, and for purposes of titillation, dresses in women's clothes and has no intention of removing his penis. Robert Stoller describes it as a way of indulging in the temptation while avoiding the danger of being "female," the arousal produced by the act being confirmation of manhood. According to Stoller, the transvestite says to himself, " 'Am I still a male, or did the women succeed in ruining me?' And the perversion—with its exposed thighs, ladies' underwear, and coyly covered crotch—answers, 'No, you are still intact. You are a male. No matter how many feminine clothes you put on, you did not lose that ultimate insignia of your maleness, your penis.' And the transvestite, or 'CD,' gets excited. What can be more reassuringly penile than a full and hearty erection?"

A transsexual (or "T") wants only to be the opposite sex and wears that sex's clothes not for a transvestite's erotic charge but to feel that she is where he belongs, or he is where she belongs. Sexual orientation will vary and may not be known until after hormones: Jennifer Boylan quotes her own therapist that one-third of male-to-female transsexuals become man-desiring heterosexuals, a third homosexual (i.e., lesbian), and another third asexual. Chevey has said that Ellen will be in the first category, but I ask him how he knows.

"You can't know definitively and you always wonder." (Here, and on other sensitive occasions, I notice my brother retreating from the confessional "I" into the impersonal "you.") "And not having had any sex with a man, you can't really be sure, other than feeling an attraction to them, but you can't get rid of your attraction to women, either."

He describes attractions that are more romantic-erotic than pointedly sexual—a movie star's sex appeal is exciting but not necessarily in a genital way. "You don't want to spread your legs but all of you is attracted to attractive people, on so many levels."

J. Michael Bailey, a psychologist at Northwestern University whose writings about the sexual fantasies of transsexuals provoked a firestorm of controversy (about which more later), made a career studying the behavior, speech, and movement of various transgender types. In his signature book, *The Man Who Would Be Queen*, citing the original findings of researcher Ray Blanchard, he describes the differences between homosexual and heterosexual male-to-females, finding the former to be extremely feminine gay men, whereas the heterosexuals were men "erotically obsessed with the image of themselves as women." He and other researchers pointed out what now seems obvious: that heterosexual male-to-females, as distinct from homosexual transsexuals, are often not very feminine. Or as Chevey says: "There are two types of transsexuals—those who grow up beautiful, with high voices, and pass easily, and other types, like me, who are just the opposite. There's no way you can hide it."

And what about recent articles on preschoolers, boys who want to dress as girls and who may or may not ultimately become gay *or* transsexual? Some of the kids go back and forth, makeup and nail polish one day, rough-and-tumble guy togs the next.

"Dressing up for me," says Chevey, "wasn't the same as for a transvestite or a drag queen. Maybe I'm splitting hairs, but it wasn't a sexual turn-on so much as the only thing you could do that would allow you to experience a little bit of your female side."

"Did you ever feel you were glad to have a penis, that it was gratifying or superior?"

"Not at all. I was just wishing I could change. And at that time there was no hope. There were no 'role models' except through the back door: I'd go to a movie like *Goodbye Charlie* with Debbie Reynolds and *Switch* with Ellen Barkin, or *Victor/Victoria* with Julie Andrews: they could take a taboo subject and, by treating it humorously, made it okay. Other people would say what a funny movie and what are we going to do this afternoon, but I would see something like that and just be lit up inside. It was the backdoor approach. That's probably a good term, because you feel ecstatic but you have to keep it to yourself. You're sitting around and somebody will mention one of those movies and you have to be careful not to let your reactions show. In the first two cases a male character had died and come back, reincarnated as a woman, as if this is the only way for society, or Hollywood, to address this problem, this fantasy of 'sex change,' and pass the censors. For me it was a sort of lifeline! I just wanted to go back and see the movie a thousand times. That was before videocassettes or DVDs. Once they came in, I could rent them. And watch them over and over. You don't realize the importance of some of these things for transsexuals."

In any case, Chevey doesn't conform to Stoller's description of a transsexual boy formed by rearing and learning, who "begins to show his extreme femininity by age two or three, though first signs may appear as early as age one." To my eyes he was all boy.

At the same time, Chevey insists, it never felt like a choice.

"Eleanor has said several times, 'You've gotten what you've always wanted.' As if it was some achievement or title or prize. The truth is that I wish transsexuality had never happened to me. From the outside it looks like a selfish act, from the inside, not at all. I had a 'happy' life before destroying it all. My life was wonderful just as it was. It's still wonderful! It's trite to say it, but I wouldn't wish transsexuality on my worst enemy. Like everyone born with a birth defect—which I believe transsexuality is—I wonder, 'Why did this have to happen to me?'"

"How did the decision come about?"

"The need is much stronger. 'Decision' is the wrong word. It has taken me many years to understand, trying to keep an open mind about what seemed important at the time, and what has come to seem so in retrospect.

"First, to do such a thing would have been totally self-destructive, emotionally and physically. In the relative tolerance of today, we simply do not remember just how hostile the environment was in 1975. Even twenty years *later*, they were still dragging gays behind pickup trucks. It would have been impossible. Crazy. The impulse to change one's sex seems irrational, but to do something about it was even more so.

"Then there was Pete. I didn't want a child but had acquiesced, and therefore I took full responsibility. He might or might not have accepted his father becoming a female, but I couldn't take that chance.

"The reaction of Mother had seemed critical at the time, but I've come to think her importance was a lesser factor. After all, I could have just disappeared, gone out to the West Coast with a new name and made a life that wouldn't have impinged on hers.

"I'd left my marriage, gone out to explore the possibilities, then the survival instinct kicked in. I backed off. As much as I wanted it, I still wanted to live. The determination, the urge and its eventual fulfillment, is not a decision so much as an addiction. So I swore I could control it. But with an addiction, there are things you can do and after a while it gets better. Not this urge. It grows and grows under the surface. You fight the urge, knock it down, it comes back. Over thirty years it takes a huge toll. I began to feel it would kill me if I *didn't* go with it. Sometimes I was just shaking, it was so stressful inside. What others call a 'decision' was a long, agonizing, soul-searching, gut-wrenching process, and the worst of it was knowing what it would do to everyone around me. I didn't think I could live with what I'd be doing to others.

"But it gets to the point that it's suicide if you *don't* do it. Whereas earlier, I felt it would be suicide to do it, now it was the reverse. Eleanor never saw the intensity. I hid it from her, so that she didn't understand; she thought if you can live with it like you've done, why can't you go on? But she had no idea of what was going on inside."

The idea that it's a "choice," at least where Chevey's concerned, seems increasingly, almost laughingly, difficult to believe when you consider all the disastrous consequences. Here, after all, is what he's facing: facial reconstructive surgery, the outcome of which no one can foretell; constantly looking over her shoulder for psychopaths so threatened by the idea they'd attack or even kill her; no way of knowing who will stand by her among family and friends; the fear of meeting, whenever she goes out, snickers, murmurs, raised eyebrows, eyes either averted or staring; the overt or subtle ostracism; outrageous expenditures of money for procedures (surgery, electrolysis, hormone patch) with no health coverage. And here's what he's giving up: all the advantages of a good marriage, the closeness, the trips, the plans, the sex, the mother-in-law, possibly the stepchildren; the perks of being a man, the automatic authority, the respect of agents, clerks, waiters, his secure place in society.

He expects to be treated like a freak. "My therapist told me about a transsexual patient of his. She went into Starbucks not too long ago, and when she was paying for her coffee, she thanked the guy at the register. 'You're welcome, *sir!*' he said with heavy emphasis."

Who would choose this? The cardinal belief among homophobic conservatives that individuals "choose" to be homosexual, with all its

disadvantages, is questionable enough, but it would be insane for anyone with a relatively secure and traditional life and lifestyle to throw it
all over for a life considered beyond the pale and whose outcome is dubious at best. "Lifestyles" and identities, in this era of rampant individu-
alism, are not totally without "choice": we may, and may often, choose
which "side" of ourselves to act upon, which to disavow. There's the
minister who chose to suppress rather than express his homosexuality,
as his Christian vocation was more important than his (as he sees it) sex
life. Cynthia Nixon angered some in the gay community when she admitted to having been married to a man, then chose to live as a lesbian.
For some, it is easier to suppress, or at least marginalize, sex drives than
for others. Nixon honestly confronted the heterosexual side that most
homosexuals rigorously deny. Even transsexuals deny their former
selves, change their birth certificates, but for them, precisely because of
the fearful consequences, the word "choice" seems a misnomer.

"Did you make mistakes," I ask him, "catch yourself in public thinking, I'm a woman, and behave differently?"

"I didn't so much think, I'm a woman, as think, I've got to act like
a man. Later there were times when I'd do something like the gesture
I just did—palms open—and I'd catch myself and think, that's female.
A man tends to show the back of his hands; the female is much more
submissive. There are little things like that, or maybe you cross your
legs in the wrong way and suddenly you realize and correct yourself.
You have your antennae up all the time."

"So you're a student of female and male behavior."

"Yes, all my life I looked at women and women's fashion. I was
aware of the way they were dressing. I think back on certain events
now, like once coming home from school, or maybe it was cotillion,
when I was in an all-girl car pool. The other boys were jeering and

envious. I played it to the hilt; it was cool that I was in the midst of all these cute girls, but at the same time I was thinking—"

"This is where I belong."

Ethel had suggested we get in touch with gay activist groups or the umbrella organization GLBT (Gay, Lesbian, Bisexual, and Transgender) National Help Center, but transsexuals are not really regarded as one of the fold. I mentioned it to my brother on the phone, after he'd gone home.

"They think of us as freaks," he said, "the same way straight people do."

How sad was this! I suppose there's a certain logic: gay males in thrall to the pleasures of the phallus would naturally be the last to identify with such self-mutilation. They simply can't understand it. (In all fairness, who can? Certainly not transsexuals.) Moreover, as political activists, gays have a hard enough time of it without incurring even more culturally dubious fellow travellers. To them, the transsexual is the crazy aunt descending on a family whose social status is none too secure to begin with. In fact, the four components of GLBT are all far more disparate than such a rubric allows for. Gays and lesbians may have less in common than either has with straight people of their respective sexes; and there are subsets and branches of each.

I tried to imagine him, her, somewhere. What about a community with other transsexuals? "I don't want to be one of them," he said. What did he even mean by this, a strangely callous remark from someone as generally empathetic as he? I assumed he meant a commune of in-your-face queerish drag queens, mascaraed babes out of *La Cage aux Folles* rather than sobersided members of society, but why, if they come from backgrounds as diverse as he makes clear they do? He was equally averse to joining an online support group. More of a recluse than a joiner, Chevey had always been obsessed with privacy (the first piece of equipment he bought when he went into business for himself was a shredder). He was so secretive, Mother and I never knew if he had any clients! Even Ethel, when I told her, was surprised at his attitude. "But he *is* one of them," she said.

I only gradually came to another interpretation. Because a transsexual thinks constantly and obsessively about being a woman, there's a tension between the need for support, on the one hand, and the desire, if not to pass completely as a woman, at least to live in as utterly normal a way as possible. The last thing they want is to wear the label "T," join a club, and be seen by the world as freaks or at best hybrids. They're already so far out on the fringe, so beyond political legitimacy, there isn't the same desire for political solidarity as among homosexuals or other minorities. Indeed, solidarity would only magnify their problems. Most want, as Chevey says, "to blend in with the heterosexual population."

This all came home to me when I watched a CNN documentary, *Her Name Was Steven*, in which Steve Stanton (now Susan), the one-time city manager of Largo, Florida, gave a lucid and dispassionate account of her feelings and decisions. Of particular interest to me was her appearance at a congress of transsexuals, where she infuriated her fellow transsexuals by refusing to toe the line and voice solidarity.

"Somehow I've been thrown into this role as a national spokesperson for a cause I don't understand myself yet," she says at one point. One applauds her courage and sees a woman quite at peace with herself. But the ex-wife is a different story. She has refused to appear in the documentary but answers questions off camera, and at one point says poignantly, "I watched him gradually fade away, and it has been like a slow death for me." Eleanor must be feeling something like this about Chevey.

I try to imagine losing Andrew in a way that is almost more complete than death, because it brings into question the shared past and the self that has morphed and mutated, but always within the endless dance of marriage.

I ask Beth if Chevey's revelation of transsexualism undermined her sense of their marriage, and she replies in the negative. They were best friends before and remain so.

"He had such integrity," she says, "more than anyone I've ever known. And so does she. Nevertheless, I hope Ellen doesn't want to talk about hair and makeup all the time. And I've told him he can't be my friend if he wears froufrou clothes. You know, over-the-top feminine—plunging necklines and short skirts." The truth is, we're all more "masculine" than he is, or rather than the she that he will be.

The one person who can no longer joke is Eleanor. They've been married twenty years, and this has upended her life. They met twenty-two years ago, when Chevey had just formed The Argonaut Company and advertised for an assistant. Not just any assistant but precisely the woman—lovely with pearly pale skin, competent, and funny—who walked through the door.

CHAPTER FOUR

My Brother Advertises for a Secretary and Reels In a Wife

Richmond Times-Dispatch, December 5, 1982:

SECRETARY/RECEPTIONIST
PART TIME

For small West End business, 9 to 1 daily. I need someone who is experienced in (or, with some tasks, willing to learn) typing, carrying logs and laying a fire, light bookkeeping, running errands, light housekeeping, taking occasional day trips, light yard work, attending nighttime classes, swatting flies, etc. If this job interests you, better see your psychiatrist. If still interested, send your complete resume, along with your explanation why you would ever want a job like this one to CA 430 c/o this paper. Be sure to let me know your needs and wants, too. Sorry, but if you smoke (tobacco), or have smoked within the last few months, save your breath. We wouldn't work well together.

*U*nderstandably (and no doubt by intention) the responses were few. The interested party had to have not only a sense of humor but a fairly peculiar one. Mother and I thought it extremely funny, though Mother also shook her head in disbelief. Not just at the wording but at the ad itself. We still didn't know if he had any clients: could he afford a secretary? We didn't quite understand that it was a coded casting call for a wife. (Now, looking over those qualifications, I wonder if it might have been an even more deeply encrypted SOS for a husband.) Chevey may have been to all appearances a conservative guy, but he did everything in his own idiosyncratic and oxymoronic way: that is, logical to the point of fanaticism, applying rationalist precepts to areas where sentiment and emotion rule. For example, when Mother was old, not yet needing full-time help, but getting fragile, and worried about living alone, she wailed, "What's going to happen if I die? I could lie there for days and no one would know."

"Well, it won't matter," said Chevey, "because you'll be dead." True, but not very diplomatic. And when he saw the square footage devoted to books and bookshelves in our New York apartment he was shocked. "You could have a grandmother live here for the space they occupy." Although there were lovely scarves and clutch purses, prominent among the gifts he gave me over the years were the practical ones: when I first moved to New York, a single girl with roommate in walk-up apartment, he gave me a fire extinguisher for Christmas; another year, an adding machine; in later years (to Andrew and me), a smoke detector (which sat on the shelf because we didn't know how to install the battery) and a scale that could be used for both postage and food. Two computer programs he gave me, Quicken and Palm Desktop, were expressions of his philosophy of money managing, his professional calling card, so to speak, laid out to every client: Keep a record of every expense. Try to forecast your expenditures for the next six months, the next year, the distant future. We know now that our expectations of the future, like our recollections of the past, are utterly irrational and miles off base, both being drawn from immediate experience, the here and now, since the future is unknowable, the past selectively remembered. So his exhortations would have been an exercise in futility, even if he hadn't been waging a battle for rationality in that most unreceptive of terrains: the mind-set of investors who want to believe in the magic of the stock market.

I loved Quicken but used it simply to balance my bank account, and, without a yearly tutorial from Chevey, could never remember at tax time how to categorize expenditures. He, of course, carried a PalmPilot at all times. We'd stop by a café for a cup of coffee and in would go the date, time, and amount. He was a wonderful teacher, endlessly patient. He occasionally taught night courses and once wrote a series of articles in a neighborhood service paper on investing. They were lighthearted admonitions like "Ten Investment Mistakes," meant to foster the idea of financial planning—how to have reserves, keep credit card debt down, maintain records, and plan for the future with actuarial probabilities in mind. That most people (1) think they will live forever or die before they run out of money, and (2) would rather do almost anything than track their expenses (a task both tedious and embarrassing: our *petites faiblesses* for junk food or shoes or booze, suddenly revealed, in irrefutable abundance, as vices and addictions), this he understood. Never mind. He'd go on counseling his clients to keep records and plan for the future, and simply hope that somewhere and in someone a seed had been planted that might one day blossom into financial circumspection. His sense of mission gave him satisfaction enough.

I often wondered how he could even understand the mental fragility of the rest of us, so resistant was he to the siren call of instant gratification. Where most of us, according to Daniel Kahneman, Nobel scientist and author of the best seller *Thinking, Fast and Slow*, are mentally crippled by "cognitive biases," decisions based on intuition and emotion that override reason, Chevey belonged to that rare minority who fall into Kahneman's second category of those who think and behave according to reason and logic. Will Ellen migrate girlishly and irrationally into category one?

He was a true Virginian in his fiscal conservatism, but his practicality was his own, a private joke among family and friends. I gave him a toast at the rehearsal dinner before his marriage to Beth, roasting him on several points, and got a knowing laugh when I ended:

"Chevey, it's Christmas Eve, we must buy a tree."
"No, we'll wait till tomorrow when we can get one for free."

He was the go-to man for computer questions from his tech-challenged harem—Eleanor, Beth, and me. He set up a DOS program on my PC whereby I could save each day's work without going through the whole set of files and documents. When Bruce, my computer guy in New York, came for some emergency, he would always recognize, with some displeasure, any little improvement (or, as he saw it, interference) from my brother. Like the wife who detects a smear of lipstick not her own on her husband's collar, he saw Chevey's fingerprint the minute he turned on the computer. But Bruce was too expensive to call for little things, so I'd telephone Chevey in Virginia and later at Pine Mountain.

"Hey, I was going to call you anyway," I'd say sheepishly, if more or less truthfully, "but I've got a little problem." I'd lost the icon bar, the formatting, the screen saver, hit the wrong key and brought down havoc, couldn't find the Gmail "Away" message (Google had changed the setting), and somehow he'd manage to fix it over the phone.

At one point, much later, my right arm is in a sling and I'm trying to write a review. I think of it not as *my* arm but The Arm, an appendage hanging from my shoulder with no relation to me. While I'm talking on the phone, The Arm lands on the backspace key and continues to backspace until the whole document is erased.

"First take your hands off the computer and sit back," he says when I call him. (It's already too late for that.) "Then go get a cup of coffee. The disaster hasn't happened yet. What's important is not what you just did, but what you do next!" And he gives me instructions for rescuing the document, which of course I'll forget and have to call him again the next time it happens.

He wasn't always so indulgent, and one of the very few times of real acrimony between us was over money. I had moved to New York and gotten a job and Mother was helping me financially. He was outraged, and wrote me a letter so blistering that it practically burned the skin off my hands. In his eyes, I was nothing more than a pampered princess who didn't have to prove myself by making my own way financially.

Back in 1978 he had just started his own company and called it The Argonaut Company, based on the famous myth of Jason and the Golden Fleece. I thought it might have something to do with Jason being a nontraditional sort of guy, less the masculine warrior-hero than a manager, more democratic, more uncertain with his crew of proven heroes. But Chevey says it was simply the idea of a quest, the search for the Golden Fleece, which could be retirement wealth, lifelong striving.

Our Jason hung out his shingle, and in answer to the ad, there on his doorstep, braving a busy intersection in Richmond's West End, arrived the heaven-sent helpmeet, Eleanor. There may have been other candidates, but he hired her immediately. She began on the first working day of January 1983. A former high-school English teacher and a divorcée (and, as it happened, several years younger than her new boss), she had the typing, shorthand, and fire-building skills required, plus the unspoken credentials of attractiveness, intelligence, and a laid-back, no-nonsense attitude. There were a few more pluses (or minuses) that weren't in the job specs even in Chevey's head: Eleanor had two small children, was a deeply religious Christian conservative (Baptist), and, to counterbalance any alarms this might raise, had a sense of humor that was on the wild side. His occasionally dark humor coincided with hers; her quickness and common sense gave him everything he needed in a secretary . . . and a great deal more.

They worked side by side, a mom-and-pop operation literalized and sanctified by marriage in 1985. Her children—Barbara, an eleven-year-old girl, and her five-year-old brother, Adam—soon warmed to Chevey completely and permanently, as did her mother. My own mother was predictably less enthusiastic. A Baptist! And coming after I had married a Greek. But she came to love Eleanor, as how could she not have? They had bought a rather plain ranch house in a woodsy neighborhood near the University of Richmond and renovated it into something beautiful. The architect they hired walked in and immediately saw the possibility of a house in the Frank Lloyd Wright style: they covered the façade with stone, landscaped the sloping front lawn, and added a high-arched sunroom with skylight and a reflecting pool in back. They continued to work together, travelled as often as they could, mostly to places within the United States and Canada. Unlike me, who seemed to have been born facing Europe, Chevey preferred Sausalito, historical places in Virginia, or places of great natural beauty, like the Pacific Northwest.

They saw each other through family crises, of which they had more than their share. On our side, Chevey had a son by Beth who never quite found his place in life and may have had Asperger's syndrome. Pete was pretty much a loner, and when he came of age he took to travelling and drinking. He was a big, blond boy, the sweetest and gentlest of creatures, though when his eyes narrowed, as they did involuntarily, his expression could become quite menacing. When he came to visit us in New York, he walked around with his pants unbelted and hanging low on the hip in homeboy style, and immediately found his way to some bars. Feeling responsible for my young nephew,

I was beside myself, but Andrew reassured me. "You should be more concerned about the other barflies," he said. "Pete looks like he's come to the city to kick some butt." One night, hoping to induce him to stay put, I ordered pizza from our favorite East Side joint—thin crust, with haute toppings like wild mushrooms, eggplant, smoked mozzarella, goat cheese, pancetta, etc. Pete took one look at it, hurried to the phone, and called Domino's, where he had a charge account.

He could be quite funny in his own way, a way that, not unlike his father's, had its own weird logic. Plus, his addictions didn't fall far from the tree of our own family, especially our mother, who was also a smoker, drinker, traveller. The trouble for Pete was he couldn't do one without the other, and by now most of the airlines had banned smoking. So he simply went to those places served by Aeroflot, the Russian airline, which still allowed smoking.

The tragedy came a few years later. Pete had gotten his own small place in Florida. He was quite proud of it and was looking forward to a visit from his grandmother, Beth's mother, who was driving down especially to see him. In preparation for her arrival, Pete became quite agitated, worried that he and his place might not be presentable. Having no social skills, no sense of ease to fall back on, he had been taking tranquilizers. The night of her arrival, he drank a good amount, and that, combined with tranquilizers, caused an accidental overdose. He died in his sleep. He was twenty-four.

Chevey, and Eleanor, too, had lived in terror that Pete would have a car accident, killing himself, perhaps killing someone else. At least that hadn't happened. It was about the only ray of redemptive light in his death and sadly unfulfilled life—or so we think. But who knows if Pete didn't get as much satisfaction from his offbeat pleasures, unable as he was to explain himself, as those of us who can communicate our desires and frustrations in a common language.

And during all this, there was yet another reason that Chevey and Eleanor waited in terror for the phone to ring. She had a large family with various problems, and in a crisis she was always the one they turned to. And there were the mercifully normal but very difficult aging and dying of our mothers, Eleanor being as sweet and attentive to mine as Chevey would be to hers.

Now, after twenty years of deeply intertwined lives, she is suddenly forced to abandon not only her vision of the future, of growing old with Chevey, but her version of the past. Of what she thought was love in every sense of the word. The marriage has to be revisited and reassessed; the past was not what she thought it was. Were the moments of intimacy completely hollow, a charade on his part? What had he been thinking of? Her sense of herself, of her own desirability, was shaken to the roots. And now, if it got out, it wasn't the humiliation she worried about, but her privacy. She thought of her family. Her two grown children—Barbara, now a dot-com executive in California, and Adam, a social worker in Richmond—were devoted to their stepfather. Her mother she simply couldn't tell. And there was her church group. They would ask why she and Chevey had broken up and what could she tell them?

And, and, and . . . so many fresh horrors to be dealt with. We worried about his future life, the dangers, the isolation. What made it all worse was how good he'd been as a husband, how kind to her family. The person who'd shared her problems was now the problem. Maybe—she prayed, I prayed—he would change his mind.

Why couldn't he just retreat to a back room and dress himself up in women's clothes? Because a "pretend" woman is not what he's after.

Though what causes it remains a mystery, one step in discrediting the idea that one can manipulate gender was the John Money scandal. In

1967, when beliefs in environmental influences were ascendant, Dr. Money was a suavely successful sex researcher connected with the pioneering efforts at Johns Hopkins Hospital in Baltimore. When the parents of a male infant who'd suffered a botched circumcision came to him for advice, he persuaded them to raise the boy as a girl under his supervision, believing that hormones would effect a successful switch to female. The experiment was a disaster, the childhood a misery as "she" acquired both male and female secondary characteristics. She later reverted to a male, but the experience haunted him through marriage and adulthood, and he eventually committed suicide. Most scandalous of all was the cover-up of the failure by Money and his fellow believers as they continued to perform such interventions, surgical and otherwise, for twenty-odd years.

I ask Chevey what he thinks. "Most of the doctors I've talked to think that it is prenatal, without knowing quite how. Which brings up an interesting point, because that really makes transsexualism a birth defect. It certainly is a birth abnormality if you think of nontranssexualism as being the norm, which it certainly is statistically; then being a transsexual is really the result of a birth defect. Now I don't think that other transsexuals would appreciate hearing that. They would want to think it is something else."

"Like what?"

"I can't really say, but my guess is they would say, 'No, no, I was supposed to be a girl all along, but came out a man.' But then what is a birth defect? Isn't that a birth defect? I don't know. You are playing with words here. The point is that it does seem to be something that happens prior to birth."

In fact, from the early either/or, nature/nurture debates, and with advances in neuroscience, has come the more sophisticated view that transsexualism is caused by a multiplicity of pre- and postnatal influences, and that probably a disturbance occurs in the time gap between the developing brain and the influx of sex hormones. But it's still speculation since no sex-atypical brain structures have been found, no specific marker for biological causes.

And even what we mean by biology is no longer clear. After all, the womb is an environmental ecosystem of its own. And are PCBs—those endocrine-disrupting chemicals found in plastic, pesticides, and food additives that can feminize the fetus—environment or biology? Many scientists have linked these chemicals with gender identity and reproductive problems. Another theory—or an additional possibility!—is that falling sperm count among human males produces transgenderism. The more we know about genes (the endless variables and variations), it seems the less we know. We do have a finer appreciation of the endless and mutually reinforcing dance of mutation and adaptation, of "born that way" and "made that way," but this "knowledge" carries with it an admission of ignorance: specific diagnoses are elusive, prescriptions for treatment even more so. That an increasing number of teenagers are deciding to change sex early on (especially girls into boys) has created a whole new set of problems and possibilities. The transition is often more successful, aesthetically and psychologically, if it occurs in youth or around puberty, but any kind of intervention at that stage (from puberty blockers to surgery) can have disastrous consequences. The brain is still evolving, the normal confusions of sex are still in a state of irresolution. If a young person's yearning to be the opposite sex turns out not to be a deep-seated and unequivocal question of identity but just the melodrama of adolescent hormones and experimentation, or an escape from something else, like depression or isolation, he or she will be stuck irreversibly on the other side. This dilemma is especially true of children. When three-

and four-year-olds demand to wear clothes of the opposite sex, there has been a growing tendency to see this as budding transsexualism and treat them with hormones. Parents should be wary since, by various estimates, only a third will prove to be transsexuals while another third will be gay, and the rest heterosexual. No one can know at this stage how their adult identities will develop, and it's too soon to make such a definitive decision about the future.

One scientist, Joan Roughgarden, believes that a large part of it comes from the moment when the baby first opens his eyes and emulates whatever person his eyes fix upon. That person becomes the baby's "tutor." Tutorial is an intriguing idea, and "degrees" is an operative word. This would fit in with the (to me) rather startling findings of psychoanalyst Susan Coates, who has written about cross-dressing among children. In studying a group of three- and four-year-olds, she found some of the males dressing in girls' clothes and traced it back to trauma between the parents, specifically a wounded mother. Something had happened in the marriage, a husband who left or was abusive. The boys were allying with the mother and trying to make reparation by dressing like her, but they didn't end up becoming transsexuals.

"At that age," Coates told me, "sexual identity is not yet stable. They're not aware of it. Show them a picture of a male and a female naked and ask which is a woman and which a man, and they'll say, 'How do I know? They don't have any clothes on!' "

"This would seem to be a subgroup," I suggested, thinking of my sibling, who didn't fit this pattern, and she agreed. There were no early signs in Chevey's behavior, and he was at least six or seven when the disorder made itself felt, in however inchoate a form.

Psychoanalyst and author John Ross, a specialist in masculinity, writes (in *What Men Want*) of small boys who, before rigidities of gender set in, display feminine traits and express a kind of "womb envy" from a sense that only women produce babies, since there's no sign of the father's contribution.

It suddenly comes to me that Chevey experienced a breakdown while Beth was in the hospital giving birth to Pete, and I ask him about it.

"Part of it was because I didn't want a child in the first place, but more than that, I had what I called 'pregnancy envy,' the feeling that I should have been the one giving birth."

CHAPTER FIVE

Who Has It Better, Men or Women?

Which is the greater ecstasy? The man's or the woman's? . . . [T]he pleasures of life were increased and its experiences multiplied. For the probity of breeches she exchanged the seductiveness of petticoats and enjoyed the love of both sexes equally.

—Virginia Woolf, *Orlando*

*A*s I comb the past for clues to my brother's female leanings, this argument stands out, a bone of contention through the years. With the fervor of a tomboy, and later buttressed by feminist argument, I maintained that of course men had the advantage. The world was essentially organized hierarchically around the idea of male supremacy. Women's opportunities were few, their status borrowed, their vocation marriage. A deeply ingrained double standard was endemic, socially, sexually, professionally. Chevey, more controversially, argued for women. They might work or not, but their place in society and even their self-esteem didn't depend on it, while men were born into the burden of proving themselves, their professional success their identity. The pressure was enormous, and to him far outweighed the excitement of work, the lure of power and distinction. He apparently wanted the right *not* to be ambitious, not to compete. Was this because I so much wanted to? And the first person he didn't want to compete with was me? At the time, I thought some of this might come from his childhood vision of male vulnerability. My father had contracted ALS when he was fifty-three. I was thirteen then, and Chevey eight. (In fact, it was about the time that he started poking around in my closet.) My little brother watched as this youthful man withered and died, while the women in his life survived and flourished. Hence, no doubt, the fury expressed in the aforementioned screed attacking me for not supporting myself, and, by implication, Mother for helping me out.

Still, I thought now—and said to him on the telephone—just you wait. See what kind of service you get when you call someone on a business matter, go to a hotel, deal with workmen, appear alone at a restaurant! And sex . . . you'll be at the mercy of some man's taste or distaste, no longer the one who chooses and initiates.

Even before Orlando posed the question as to whose is the greater ecstasy, possibly the first known expert in these matters was the fabled Tiresias, who had lived as both man and woman. Jove and Juno were having a heated dispute as to which sex had more fun in bed, and called in Tiresias to settle the argument.

In Ovid's version, Jove, like my brother, argued for women, advancing a similar argument but in sexual terms. The wily and indefatigable god who never lost an opportunity to seduce, rape, and ravish had the gall to whine, "[W]omen have more joy / In making love than men; we do the work, / While you have all the fun." Tiresias agreed and, in her fury, Juno struck him blind. Yet for all that supposed female *jouissance*, Tiresias, when given the opportunity, chose to return to being male.

Many have evoked Tiresias to express the longing we all must feel at some moment to be the other sex. Christopher Hitchens alluded to the myth in his eloquent and sexually ambidextrous memoir *Hitch-22*:

"I would seriously like to know what it was like to be a woman, but like blind Tiresias I would also like the option of remaining myself if I wished." So we have the vicarious consolations of art and myth . . . and books and movies, and even movie stars, with whom we identify regardless of sex, or rather, precisely because of sex, since we can "be" both or either at the moment of watching.

Shape-shifting and the slipperiness of gender have never been more astutely and wittily explored than in Ovid, the renegade, the champion of women and pleasure against the stern patriotism of Virgil and the repressive hypervirility of Augustus Caesar. In one story, Jove, in order to seduce the lovely young Arcadian Callisto, disguises himself as Diana, the girl's idol. It works. Says Callisto: "Hail, goddess whose deep spell on me is greater / Than Jove's himself." And Jove's disarming response: "Jove laughed at being preferred above himself" and gave her "tongue to tongue, a most immoderate kiss."

Poor Callisto, no longer a virgin, is banished by Diana; then Juno, whose jealousy is "forever on the boil," whose sex is sublimated into wrath, turns her into a bear. But the point is that for Callisto, Diana exerts a greater spell than Jove's. Brandon Teena, according to the girlfriends Dunne interviewed for his article, exerted the same feminine appeal. He was sensitive to their needs and able to play mother, sister, boyfriend, and father to these damaged souls.

Will we prefer Ellen-*herself* to John-*himself*? Isn't there an even deeper lesson here: that the *she*-Jove is more attractive to women than the *he*-Jove? And wasn't this what made my brother so lovable—all those she-qualities he possessed? While I was too far away to be useful, he was wonderful with Mother, spoiled her when she was healthy and vital, acting as unpaid accountant and a great deal more, and then, when she grew ill and finally housebound with emphysema, he had been in constant attendance, arranging for caretakers, visiting, watching over her.

I ask him about this empathy.

"When I would be walking along with a girlfriend or woman friend, whether you're having a cup of coffee or enjoying a party or getting in and out of a car or having intercourse, you're thinking you're inside her mind, thinking what she's feeling and understanding what she needs."

"And women responded to you?"

"Yes, I think so, even if they didn't understand why. But obviously I was more interested in who they were. I was never into male bonding. I was interested in all aspects; it helped a lot in sex, but really in all aspects. Of course there are other men who are 'into' women that way, and I'm not saying I was perfect at it, but then every woman is different and you don't have an automatic window where everything's clear. But at least you realize different ways of looking at things and interpreting things. So while I don't exactly know what she needs or wants, at least I know I want to try and understand."

In a sense, the transsexual proves by his/her ability to emotionally identify with both sexes that he's the exception to the rule, the "hybrid" that both confirms and challenges the divide between male and female, between masculine and feminine. Sexual stereotypes—genetic or environmental? Hardwired or mutable? What's "natural" or "normal" in one culture may be anathema in another. A redhead in Poland is considered good luck, but redheads are bad luck in Corsica, and in Egypt they are burned. So important is a melodious singing voice in Wales that those who can't sing are ostracized. Epileptics are felt to be possessed by sacred spirits among the Hmong in Laos. In Western cultures, dating back to the Greeks, effeminacy in males has been seen as a disease, a perversion, whereas in a South American country an androgynous male can have godlike powers, uniting male and female, like the "two-spirit" people of some Native American tribes. Male and female may signify opposites to us, but in China, "yin" and "yang" mean an ultimate merger. There is ritualized transvestism in Bali, whereas in the West, drag is most often either broadly comical (hetero men in dresses) or disturbingly beautiful, like the divas of the "ball culture" in the documentary *Paris Is Burning.*

To these normative fixed poles of Western culture, however, resistance has run like an underground river, expressing itself in myths of hybrids and hermaphrodites, in art and mythology, that test, tease, and destabilize our sexual certainties. The sexual burlesques of Aristophanes and Euripides, raucous travesties of hypermasculinity, and the plays of Shakespeare reveal earlier artists and audiences more comfortable with jokes about virility and send-ups of sexual stereotypes. Like Ovid, from whose fables he so often drew, Shakespeare, the grand master of sexual paradox, appreciates the crisscrossing of not only male and female characteristics but interspecies as well. See, for example, Bottom the ass making love to Titania in *A Midsummer Night's Dream*; Beatrice and Benedick, the screwball opposites of *Much Ado About Nothing*, speaking and mocking the artificial language of courtship, exposing the obligatory nature of male-female roles. The fact that men, or boys, played women only added extra layers to the pun, with *As You Like It* and its Russian-doll roundelay of sexual disguise—a man dressed as woman dressed as man—the ultimate joke on gender.

In his emphasis on artifice and role-playing, on life as theatre, Shakespeare is the great poet of straying gender, understanding the degree to which our sexual myths and stereotypes are far from natural but are culturally created, thus susceptible to changing fashion. But the role reversals, the upending of stereotypes, the lure of regression may speak to an audience's fears as well as desires. Such violations of "nature" and order, including passion itself, are fraught with peril for the afflicted/liberated characters. The danger, Ovid understood, is that once we leave our secure perch, once Io becomes a cow, Callisto a bear, Viola a man, Bottom an ass, we will be neither one thing nor the other, will be unable to communicate with either side, and will tumble into a void of indeterminacy.

Religion provides us with other wildly differing precepts and prohibitions. Christianity believes in the sacredness of the soul and the profanity of the body: sex got its bad reputation when the church, defining itself in opposition to Judaism, formalized the association between Eve and carnality. Judaism, by contrast, placed its faith, more literally, in the human body, the here and now. The body was sacrosanct, death should be followed (almost immediately) by burial rather than cremation. So it finds itself in a Talmudic bind where the anatomically correct transsexual is concerned.

Since it's evident from the outset that male and female can't contain the "whole diverse panoply of genders and gender identities," Lori Lefkovitz suggests we reread a passage of Genesis—*zachar u'nikevah*—not as " 'God created every human being as either male or female,' but rather 'God created human kind male and female and *every combination in between.*' "

The religions align in the belief that the way things are is the way they have to be. Until times change and religious authority wanes. Once, the definition of marriage as the union between a man and a woman was as fixed and impregnable as the Rock of Gibraltar; now the marital vows are being extended, state by state, to partners of the same sex.

The perversities of religious law and superstition (are they not the same thing?) are nowhere more evident than in the interpretation of the Koran in present-day Iran. Under its current policy, homosexuals are condemned, even executed, while the state not only accepts trans-sexuals but provides money for surgery. Documenting this remarkable anomaly is the film *Be Like Others*, showing us individuals in the course of sex change (some to escape the dangers of homosexuality).

The Koran explicitly condemns homosexuality as an evil, whereas there is nothing in it that forbids transsexualism, and the Ayatollah Khomeini even issued a fatwa permitting sex changes. According to one story, a transsexual female stormed the Ayatollah's compound, opened up her top, and declared herself a woman who needed help. Khomeini said, "Woman, put on a chador. Cover yourself. You're disgraceful." And the woman said it was the happiest moment in her life.

At a transsexual support conference in Tehran the speaker is an imam who reaffirms Khomeini's dictum that transsexualism is not a sin unless so stated in the Koran. People argue that it's unnatural, says the theologian, that it changes God's natural order, but, he continues, we take wheat and turn it into flour and turn that into bread.

And so does the definition of what's "natural" change in the eye of the beholder and of holy writ.

And what about hormones? Rather than a clear-cut battle—testosterone versus estrogen—the picture is considerably more mixed. It's not that testosterone isn't a marker for male aggression, risk taking, playing with guns and fire engines, even looking at women in a certain way: it is.

A friend in Canada dropped in on a fellow scientist, a patient in a Toronto hospital, who'd been given estrogen for his disease. He was heterosexual but noted that he felt like a different person on the hormone, began looking at women's faces rather than their breasts, listening to them rather than waiting to take over the conversation.

Chaz Bono, Cher's daughter-now-son, appears in a documentary about his transition. One can't help but suspect, and he partly confirms, that this pudgy child of anorexic celebrity parents—parents who trotted her out onstage with them—simply wanted to get out of that humiliating body. The new Chaz not only looks masculine as he proudly exposes his surgically flattened chest but has changed psychologically: he is, he says, less tolerant of gossip (compare this to the now gossip-loving Jan Morris) and is more interested in machinery and male-type gadgets. He has also, by his own and his female partner's admission, lost some of "her" niceness and empathy in the process.

And it's not that estrogen doesn't make girls into sympathetic, supportive emotional figures who play with dolls and teacups: it does. But the overlap is perhaps even more significant. In fact, women do produce testosterone (men in their testicles, women in their ovaries and adrenal glands), but far less than men. Women injected with testosterone develop male characteristics, like deeper voices, facial hair, and even baldness. Tomboys have higher levels of testosterone, as do their mothers. To make matters more interesting, research connects higher testosterone to working women, and this characteristic is passed on to their daughters! I fully believe that something in my mother—her repressed ambition, her analytic mind, maybe a high level of testosterone—was passed on to me.

There is, at least for now, one area—sports—where fudging is impossible, and where we see biological determinacy at its starkest and most unforgiving; but even that is changing under the pressure of those who argue that the subjective sense of self should be the determining factor. I remember well the outrage caused by Renée Richards;

in clubs all over the country, queasiness and unease took the form of dire predictions: male players who ranked below the top 20 or 30 would change sex in order to compete in the women's game. Didn't happen. Jennifer Boylan has argued that how one identifies oneself should be the deciding factor. I wonder if Chevey agrees and ask him about it during a phone conversation.

"No, I don't. They have to make a determination, and genetic testing isn't it, but it has to be done, maybe by muscle mass, strength, speed. If someone has a clear preponderance of masculine traits, it's like steroids. It gives an unfair advantage."

Chevey was never an athlete, but it was because he had a bad eye. I ask about testosterone, did he have feelings of aggression?

"I was never the sort of timid Clark Kent type but not some big brute of a guy wanting to smash heads, either."

In a later recorded interview, we get into the specifics of sex: a subject so fraught, yet it's strange how natural these conversations have come to seem. "What about a sex drive; did you have one, or not that much?"

"I think I did. I think I was a very good lover. I always made sure."

"Did you want to date girls?"

"Yes, I loved them as friends as well as potential sexual partners. I think that's true of men as well, although they may never get enough credit in that area.

"It's hard to know what is typical; nobody talked about it, or if they did they lied. But in my early teenage years, I think I had—I know I had—strong feelings of both male and female, boy and girl. I wasn't the stereotype transsexual who felt totally female. And this is turning out to be a major aspect of my life. I was attracted to both girls and boys and naturally I didn't understand any of this. I thought, Am I gay? Of course even then—we use the term 'gay' now—we didn't use it then. All those song lyrics—'Don we now our gay apparel'—you can't sing them, the word has been totally corrupted. It's like so many things: it's hard to go back and remember how it was, we've learned so much since then. I certainly didn't know the term 'bisexual' then. A lot of people say there's no such thing as bisexual, but I don't agree." I ask him if he masturbated.

"Yes, a lot—and eventually I could only ejaculate by picturing myself as a woman. When I loved and made love to a woman, I identified with her, but I also wanted to give her pleasure. I tried so many times to change my mental image but I was just never able to."

"Did you ever try aversion therapy?"

"Not officially, but for many years, every time I was going to make love to Eleanor, I would say to myself over and over, 'You will not imagine yourself a woman, you will not imagine yourself as a woman.' But then I couldn't perform. The only way I could, and give her pleasure, was by picturing myself as a woman. And don't forget that in a long relationship, couples start fantasizing other lovers, movie stars, whatever."

"But where's the male in your scenario?"

"The person I'm touching is the male. If you're a male having sex with a female, and I think a female might say the same thing, the penis could belong to either one. You can't really tell who it's attached to. You close your eyes, there's no light in the room, and it's very easy to get lost. Most people don't think about that."

Or, I think, maybe they know but repress it. Because somehow the act of sex shatters boundaries we need to keep in place. By idealizing sex as "making love," we can retain the idea of our unique male and female individuality. But we're merged, more like e. e. cummings's girlboys and boygirls.

Chevey thus confirms what the transsexual community went to

great lengths to deny: the theory, advanced by Michael Bailey, of *auto-gynephilia* (i.e., having an erotic obsession with the image of oneself as a woman).

The term, which made Bailey anathema to the transsexual community, was from psychologist Ray Blanchard's study of a man who hadn't cross-dressed but had fantasized himself as a naked woman having sex with a man. Bailey's book, designed for the general public, brought down the wrath of the transgender community in particularly vicious terms.

I can understand the resistance to the concept, if not the venom of the attack. The image smacks of Narcissus, even a betrayal of the sexual partner, which makes it hard to accept. Also it's a reminder of the dark side of sex, the aloneness at the moment of climax, and the fact that there's a certain amount of autogynephilia in all of us, as well as curiosity about what it's like to be the opposite sex.

This is a fantasy that may be stronger in some than in others. One of the most fascinating revelations in recent Hemingway studies (or rather, insights that have emerged from a less protective view of material already available) is a more precise understanding of the "dark side" he often wrote about. Details accumulate in both the novels and the life, like the recurring hair fetish. In *A Farewell to Arms,* Lt. Frederic Henry describes the erotic charge he receives watching Catherine have her hair done (his voice becomes "a little thick from being excited"), and she wants them to cut their hair the same lengths, so they can be "just alike."

Catherine: "I want to be you."
Henry: "We're the same one."
Catherine: "At night we are."

Similarly, in the early days in Paris as described in *A Moveable Feast*, Ernest and Hadley, at his urging, grew their hair long together; throughout his marriages and friendships he urged his women to dye, cut, or otherwise change their hair, and supervised the process, even dying his own hair red in a moment of stress. Both Ernest and Mary Hemingway, his last wife, wrote about her wanting to become a boy, and about the sex games they played in which she was the boy and he the girl. What Hemingway considers a dangerous loss of identity is reimagined in his posthumously published novel *The Garden of Eden*, when another Catherine cuts and cuts her hair and changes and changes ("I'm a girl, but I'm a boy too and I can do anything and anything and anything"), and when, in the dark of their lovemaking, the writer-protagonist becomes Catherine, and says, "Now you can't tell who is who, can you?"

For Hemingway such deviancy was a "corruption" that gradually corrodes the self. And ends—at least for Catherine—in madness. Gregory (Gigi), Hemingway's third son (he wanted a daughter), was considered the most talented of Hemingway's children, the most like his father, and also, in the words of Gigi's son John Hemingway, the "black sheep of the family." In *Strange Tribe*, John describes his father's mental instability, his manic-depression, and the cross-dressing that began when he was ten years old. Although Gigi married several times, and even worked as a doctor, he was more often adrift and living in ramshackle style. He was arrested several times for dressing as a woman in public. His father reported that it was for "drug abuse," and felt that the scandal of Gigi's first arrest in a Los Angeles movie theater had killed his mother, Pauline, Hemingway's second wife. Finally, as Gigi's life spiraled downward, he underwent a sex change—which solved nothing. He, now she, wound up dead in a Miami jail, wearing women's clothes.

Father and son were both heterosexual, passionate lovers of women, and yet both had a strong female side that Hemingway père was at least able to ventriloquize in his novels. Hemingway's theatrically hypermale image and legend can be seen as a defense against fear—fear not just of the woman in himself, but of the women in his life, the Others whom he so needed and depended on. (There were four wives and no gap: each wife-to-be supplanted her predecessor before the marriage was over.)

One reason Hemingway endures, like his rival, enemy, and friend F. Scott Fitzgerald, is the palpable sense of vulnerability, a nakedness he exposes to the world. Hemingway's brave and edgy flirtation with the darkness of transvestism speaks to the longing and fear in all of us of losing the self in the other, of merging until we disappear.

I think of Chevey and me as children, both trying to kiss our elbows. Then I think of us as teenagers, each standing alone before a mirror. (Which of us is the "real" girl?) We have as yet but the dimmest idea of sex or "sexual identity." We've read books, watched movies, memorized certain images, and are gradually assembling the bits and pieces of imaginary adult selves. We kiss the mirror (my lover/my self), pose, apply makeup, try on different dresses (the same ones?), practicing for the lovers we hope will come to tell us who we are.

CHAPTER SIX

My Brother Writes a Story

"*T*he worst thing about it," says my analyst friend Ethel Person, "is you discover you don't know the person you thought you knew." Later, others will express a similar opinion. One man in his fifties tells me that if his brother suddenly came to him with the revelation that he was transsexual or homosexual, he'd be furious, wondering why his sibling hadn't trusted him enough to tell him before.

Such feelings are understandable, possibly even typical, but they are not mine. I was perfectly content—to my shame, I guess—not to have known of this until now. More important, I never thought I *knew* Chevey. In general, I'm rarely surprised when a person behaves in a way considered "out of character." We are a rotating cast of aspects of self that are shown to one person, or in one setting, and hidden in another. Memorial services are often jarring in this regard: friends and relatives eulogize the deceased in such conflicting terms they might be talking of different people.

The nice boy next door turns out to be a serial killer, yet there are usually clues that we've chosen to ignore. And my ruling assumption is we can never know another person, *especially* if that person is close to us. It's why I love detective stories: the revelation that the murderer was the patient secretary, the charming brother-in-law! In *Law & Order* wives and husbands kill each other; parents think they know their children (our daughter *couldn't* be a lap dancer!) but don't. We're simply blinkered by proximity and, in families, by the roles that have become hopelessly ingrained through some witches' brew of choice, need, collusion, and coercion. We go away, spend thousands on therapy, think we've escaped; then we come back for the holidays and the old wounds open like bivalves in steam. All it takes is one drop of alcohol, one skeptical glance, and the hard-won insights of years on the couch—the illusion of mastery of one's life—evaporate in a flurry of insults and recriminations!

One day, when Chevey and I were adults, we were talking with Mother about our perceptions of each other. Chevey, with barely concealed anger, told us we didn't know him at all. "My friends think I'm very funny," he said, and Mother and I looked at each other with barely concealed surprise. Chevey, funny? And yet it turns out to be true: he is. Or rather, should I say *she* is? It is only in recent years that I've realized how funny my sibling can be. Was he always, and I just didn't know it? Friends often know us better than our families do, and casual friends—more detached, less sensitive—may actually see us more clearly than close friends. Intense friendships almost by definition reproduce the distorted patterns of family ties, whereas we all know the relief of spilling our guts to a stranger on a plane. In any case, our later years have been filled with laughter, distilled reminiscences of the past, rippling onward to the absurdities and vexations of the present, not least of which is his migration from male to female. But if Chevey hid his sense of humor from his family, how much else? And what, reciprocally, did I hide? Do we not learn in the terrible scrutinizing intimacy of family how to become artists of disguise? Sometimes, as children, as teenagers, and beyond, we don't know each other because we are not there to be known.

In childhood, he was simply the much younger brother, parachuting into my only-child paradise. For a full two years, in 1943 and '44, Mother and I enacted a nightly ritual. Kneeling together on the floor beside my bed, we prayed for a brother or sister for me. This was to encourage God to provide, of course, but also to forestall jealousy. When he appeared in 1945 I naturally took some credit for the miracle birth, but the novelty soon wore off. As a doll-averse, nonmaternal type, I couldn't take a motherly interest, and as a pal, he showed no promise whatsoever. He was always so much younger, displaying what I took to be boyish traits: ornery, cute, irritating, smart-alecky, with childhood handicaps I was meant to feel sorry for (bad ears, bad eyes). He was stubbornly oppositional and got the nickname "Vice-a-Versa" for contradicting everything anyone said. He claims it sprang from a need to consider both sides to a question, now a virtue but then an irritant, like a gnat always biting back.

When I look at snapshots in a family photograph album, the little boy who's Chevey is utterly mysterious to me—but then so is the older sister Molly standing beside him. He's about six, she, eleven, they're living at the farm, ten miles outside of Richmond in Goochland County. In 1948, when I was eight and Chevey three, we moved into Ashley, an 1890s white frame farmhouse on the crest of a hill. It sat atop 230 acres of what had until recently been a working tenant farm. There was a tenant house, a barn (with sleepover hayloft), pigs and chickens, dogs, and also Uncle Charlie, the grizzled old black retainer who came with the property and lived in a cabin at the bottom of the hill. Our parents, amateur architects, had the façade covered in brick and added a wing. Molly and Chevey are playing or posing in the yard that extends from the flagstone terrace and overlooks grazing pasture and woods. In a few years, that yard will give way to a swimming pool, created for the pleasure of family and friends, but especially in the hope of attracting boys (armed with new driver's licenses) who might otherwise not court the teenage girl who lives so far from the city.

Moving to this farm was a long-standing dream of my father's. He had married late, worked in various jobs relating to mortgage and real estate. He loved land, the sight and feel of it, but hated working for other people (a phobia Chevey and I would inherit), and had finally found himself professionally when he started his own realty mortgage business. He worked hard; there were lean years, but the farm was a sanctuary. We rented out several acres of pasture land for grazing, and Daddy loved nothing better than to come home, put on his old clothes, mount the green John Deere tractor with one of us in tow, and survey his green realm, dotted with beautiful Black Angus. In the photographs, Chevey is squatting over the new puppy and grinning adorably, while Molly cradles a kitten in her arms and looks sullen with preadolescent self-consciousness. He has his hand on the puppy's head and draws un-diluted pleasure from the contact, while she is torn between the urge to nuzzle the kitten and the social imperative of arranging herself for the camera's eye. In separate snapshots taken at the same time, he is stand-ing in shorts and shirt, his belly thrust forward and a look of mutinous defiance on his face. She simply looks awkward, inhabiting some limbo of not-yet-formed identity (now called "middle childhood"), both resist-ing and slyly acknowledging the self-display that will soon become her vocation. If you had to pick one for a bumpy passage into adulthood, it would be the girl. But that's deceiving, too. They're waiting for the im-portant things to happen, not knowing that so much of their road map has been laid out in advance, and the invisible tentacles of history have already begun closing in on them.

But what makes photographs disturbing is they challenge our illu-sion of a continuous, known self. They're often all we have of our younger selves, and yet what do they tell us? They conceal more than they reveal and become a kind of embalming that serves not so much as a trigger to the memory as an unreliable image, frozen in time.

It's not that I don't "recognize" them—I've seen the photographs often enough to know they're of my brother and me. Still, the children in these photographs are as inscrutable as my grandmother and grandfather posed formally in Victorian dress in the yellowing, dignified, standard family portrait of its time. Or Mother and my father in a candid shot from 1940 or '41, standing under a huge magnolia tree at Winterlaken, the family home in Fayetteville. While he is stationed in Alabama, Mother and I (recently born) are living in this grand old mansion (once a boys' school) that was her childhood home and is now occupied by Granny and other relatives. Daddy is on leave from his army post in Gadsden, Alabama, immaculately handsome in uniform; she's a picture of composed reserve in tailored suit and white blouse. I can conjure up Winterlaken in an instant by the smell: the magnolia trees, pine needles, a rubbery scent that might be the turpentine being extracted from trees by a process my grandfather invented. But who are these parents of mine, younger than I could ever have imagined? A happily reunited young married couple, or one already vexed by the war, a new child, tension between the young husband and his in-laws? How can I know them when they can hardly know themselves? Or rather, when such a concept has not yet acquired currency. Their notions of identity are quite different from ours, more attached to role and class, family and society, imposed at birth. Individual fulfillment? Not a term in my mother's vocabulary, though something gnaws away at her, a yearning antithetical to marriage and motherhood, a yearning that has no name. They live in a world of obligations and duty rather than rights and autonomy, of parceling themselves into inherited roles: father, army major, young husband, new father, uncertain as to what he will do when the war is over. Mother, the dancing girl and artist, saddled overnight with the frightening new job of "parenting," and worried, too, about the future.

As a child, Chevey was somewhat sickly, with one bad eye and a persistent sinus infection in the ear, preventing him from participating in sports. But he loved the farm, exploring in the woods. Separately or together, we would go down to the tricklet of a stream beside which nested Uncle Charlie's cabin, where the door was always ajar. Both ancient and ageless (he could have been seventy or ninety), he by now just puttered about doing odd jobs, cleaning out the pigpen, gathering eggs and vegetables, grabbing or hunting an occasional bird, cooking and sustaining himself. He was also our storytelling Uncle Remus. We'd sit on the floor of his cabin, an airless box, cozy and rank, the woodstove lit summer and winter. It stank most wonderfully of fumes, tobacco, wet denim—his overalls so stiff with grease and the occasional hosing down, they could have stood upright in the corner. And he would spin stories of other times, scare us with tall tales of animals and monsters, both real and imaginary. The escaped convicts from the "state farm," a penitentiary a few miles away, were real enough, and possibly no less monstrous than flying snakes.

It was in the country, too, that Chevey began to be enamored of guns after our father taught us to shoot. We would go down in the front yard, put beer cans on the fence, and fire away with a .22 rifle. Or compete in skeet-shooting competitions on the lawns of friends in Goochland County. At this we both became fairly expert, thanks to our father's instruction, and it was a sport for which Chevey needed only one good eye. He had his own BB gun and later became a gun collector. As adults, he and his "gun buddy" Karl would drive to shows all over Virginia and farther, where they would set up a table, buy and sell guns that fitted their own area of interest.

I try to square the idea of this little marksman, who seemed "all boy," with the kid harboring secret desires to be a girl and giving my wardrobe the occasional whirl.

Well, after all, while he was dolling himself up and admiring himself in the mirror, turning himself into a female artifact, so was I!

While he was confused about himself and his desires, my identity was forming around several conflicting stereotypes, male and female. One minute I was a tomboy, vowing to my car pool that I would never wear lipstick. And my favorite song was the country dirge "I Never Will Marry." I went through what I take to be the usual adolescent girl's crushes on camp counselors and gym teachers, but we possessed only the dimmest sense of same-sex love and it was confined to the context of our all-female institution. We had the Modern Library volume of Lillian Hellman plays and immediately read the one that wasn't assigned, *The Children's Hour.* And the novel *The Well of Loneliness* made the rounds, samizdat-style, and was discussed in snickering tones. We had a word—"pansy" (incorrect, of course)—for creepy teachers who left their hand on your shoulder for too long. Another girl and I practiced kissing, an episode she remembers with some embarrassment, but to me it was always in preparation for the "real thing." I felt no electric charge, nothing like the shock, six months or a year later, when a boy I liked was pursuing me in the quarry and his leg brushed against mine. Or when we played spin the bottle at parties. Then, and it seemed like just minutes after declaring my aversion to makeup and all things feminine, I was wearing an outlandish amount of lipstick, even for the fifties. I'd upgraded my wardrobe—a boon for Chevey, no doubt—to pretty, girly clothes. What did he go for? The white net dress with the blue trim (my favorite) or the blue-gray taffeta that was Mother's favorite? (It had no ruffles, something I as a "big" girl was not supposed to wear; the other did.) Otherwise it was skirts and Shetland sweaters and circle pins, the uniform. We were having that ritual of families everywhere, little sister borrows big sister's clothes, but who knew?

. . . .

I ask him how he felt about his "cross-dressing."

He says it's hard to know *what* he felt *when*.

"Again, people constantly ask, When did you first realize you were transsexual? And the answer to that is fairly recently, simply because there was no such thing as a transsexual. It's very difficult to erase what you've learned now that we have all this knowledge, or at least awareness. All I knew was I didn't want to get caught trying on your clothes."

Did he ever have "guy" ambitions like being a fireman or even a farmer?

"One of the things about me, there was no particular thing I wanted to do. I didn't know what to do with my life. Or even what to major in at college. So I took one subject in every department, an extremely varied college curriculum, hoping something would light a fire."

I think about our old dispute over "Who has it better, the man or the woman?" Chevey saw from what now seems to me a precociously young age that he didn't want a life dominated by work. So what seemed like a "lack" of ambition was a more considered "antiambition," a refusal.

But if Chevey had no single ambition, I, on the contrary, was a revolving door of them—or rather "hobbies," since ladies didn't have ambition. Mine took various forms, consonant with my multiplying and consolidating selves. I knew I wanted to become "something" when I grew up, not just a wife and mother. Mother always encouraged my independence while at the same time pushing me toward an advantageous marriage. Were the two compatible?

"My problem," she once confessed to me, "is I've always been drawn in too many different directions." This moved me deeply, possibly because I shared her dividedness. Suppose she had passed up marriage for painting, she said to me at a later time, and then didn't make a success of it. Then, as she saw it, she'd have nothing. She had had a long and varied and, in her own words at the end, "wonderful" life, but there was also a well of regret, of something missed. How else could her life have been otherwise, given the conventional, even Victorian, upbringing she had, and whose values still shaped my childhood world?

My sense of myself formed around the concept of tomboy. What that meant to me was not that I was a transsexual who wanted to be male, certainly not a "man," but more a Peter Pan–like creature, androgynous, with all of the advantages of boyhood, none of the restraints of girlhood. I no more wanted a penis than I wanted any other sign of sexual development (breasts definitely included).

So my dreams took the form of whichever "hobby" I was currently mad about: dancer, rider, preacher, actress.

In 1954 or '55, while I pass from tomboy-ballerina-preacher to girl-with-dates (the swimming pool is accomplishing its mission), and Chevey is beginning to experience odd and inexplicable urges, our father is told he has MS. It is actually the far deadlier ALS, but either the doctors haven't diagnosed it correctly or they want to give him "positive" news. So, to cope with what we think is a long-term degenerative but nonfatal illness, we move back to the city, to a house better suited to accommodate his disability. In fact, he will die two years later, in 1957, having rarely set foot outside the bedroom. It is at this point that each of us has our breakdown/breakaway. Chevey "acts out" by misbehaving, staying out all hours doing who knows what, becoming a borderline delinquent. Mother finds out his nocturnal activities include shooting out streetlights with a BB gun and setting off time-delayed cherry bombs all around West End Richmond. Feeling that she can no longer control him, she sends him away to prep school, for which he's furious, vowing revenge.

Chevey is so unhappy away from home that after three years Mother finally allows him to return to Richmond, where he will finish out at Thomas Jefferson, an excellent public high school.

At a later point, going through memorabilia, when Chevey has become Ellen, we find among the family letters and photographs a 1963 copy of the Thomas Jefferson literary magazine. It contains a short story called "One Brief Moment" written by John Haskell—who would have been eighteen and in the graduating class—in compliance with an assignment whose nature she can no longer remember. I'm astonished when I read it. Little more than a vignette, it's a delicately observed, play-by-play account of a spider building its web only to have it carelessly brushed into oblivion by a passing farmer. For three-fourths of the story the spider methodically builds the web, tests it, then walks to the outer edge of the leaf, and, still emitting "a continuous stream of webbing from his abdomen, he lowered himself over into nothingness." He waits for a gust of wind to blow him onto a neighboring tree and then, after several attempts and failures, gains a footing, then the Sisyphean struggle all over again until he has a scaffolding, then on to the second stage, weaving back and forth to complete the task. There's a description of the beauty of the sun glinting on the finished web, which "the spider never noticed . . . for to him the web was his home, his entire existence since the web caught the very food which he ate."

Then a break and the expletive "Damn it!" uttered by the hulking man who crashes "murderously through the silken threads, his huge frame ripping them into millions of pieces." But ten seconds after the domi-cide, when the wind has carried away the last fragments of his home, the spider without hesitation resumes his work, hurrying "back to the base of the leaf where he began emitting the soft, delicate, silken thread which would soon become his new home."

The tale is remarkable for the quality of its writing (lyrical, precise, a tad overlush in the manner of a beginning writer), and for the stoicism implied in the sympathy dispassionately split between the heroic travail of the spider and the no less inevitable and headlong march of the farmer-intruder: nature and man, coexisting and colliding. But of course the spider, allied with Nature as female, is the "hero," the one who remains camouflaged, vulnerable, yet determined. In this parable of persistence against mighty odds, we can see the pupate Ellen, living like the spider in an ephemeral dream home, always menaced by overbearing masculinity. But the extraordinary care and meticulousness of the story, of the spider, of Chevey, also suggest the perfectionism behind his hatred of writing.

I was still in middle school, pondering the options of matrimony (or not), acting in school plays, but with an eye to the future. From dancing to preaching, my need to perform, to get attention, now turned to acting, a pursuit that became more intense after my father died, since he had made clear his disapproval of such a career. At about the same time—can it be coincidental?—Chevey was playing with guns one day and impersonating the Virgin Mary the next.

He was attending St. Christopher's, the brother school to St. Catherine's, and it was their annual nativity play. Chevey, about ten or eleven, was chosen to play the Virgin Mary, and he looked beautiful, covered in the white hood and blue robe so that only his face showed, gentle and meditative. In essence, there was nothing particularly unusual about "cross-dressing" in parochial schools. At St. Catherine's, I was tall and got to play the lead in Shakespeare's *Julius Caesar* and Jack/Ernest in *The Importance of Being Earnest*. But what had struck me at the time, and now made sense, was not just how beautiful he looked as the Virgin Mary, but how unembarrassed, even proud, he was, and the pleasure he took when we praised him for it.

When I ask Chevey now, he says, "It was exhilarating, one of the high points of my life, getting to play a female, and legitimately!" And, looking at the pictures of him, I think it was more than the features, the feminine apparel, that made the sight of him so convincing. There was some radiant inner light that expressed itself through Mary.

It reminds me of a beautiful passage in *Conundrum*, in which Jan Morris describes how, as James, he regularly attended (and sang in the choir of) the cathedral-like Christ Church at Oxford. In its vaulting splendor and celebration of the Virgin Mary, the young James felt his own growing sense of the superiority of the female sex.

I ask Chevey how he was feeling during these years.

"I remember once I hit puberty doing a little bit of dressing. It could really be terrifying to go into a store and buy women's clothing, so I basically didn't—except maybe at Christmastime, when you could pretend it was for your sister or mother. Once I was at a friend's house and I got hold of a girl's bathing suit and tried it on, but the opportunities were few. I don't know what other transsexuals are like—this keeps coming up and I'll say it again and again—but we have this stereotype usually created by some of the most outspoken but not necessarily typical transsexuals. It was obviously a confusing time.

"I was always trying to play up the male side, not so far as Alpha Male but just 'normal.' I had to hide the feelings of being a girl. It was just socially mandated, a fate worse than death. Not easy now, coming out of the closet, but it was just terrifying back then. I joked about how transsexuals are the best actors in the world; they have to be spies. You could get killed."

Mildred Brown and Chloe Rounsley write about boys who envy girls for their clothes, their dresses, and hate their own penises, even suppress the bulge. I ask him if he can relate to that.

"I had the former, but not the latter. I thought I should be able to wear what girls were wearing but I never turned against my penis. Nor did I have a sense of female superiority. Both sexes had their advantages."

He tells me of a watershed moment, in about 2001 or '02, when he was suddenly taken aback and felt viscerally his indefinable but unbridgeable difference from the sex into which he'd been born, a moment that, perhaps not coincidentally, involved guns. He'd been invited by an acquaintance, who was trying to do something for a client, to a sporting clays event, a fund-raiser at Shirley Plantation on the river.

"Sporting clays is related to but more challenging than skeet shooting, where clay targets are projected in an open field. In sporting clays the targets are projected in a wooded section that represents what hunting's actually like, with underbrush, forest, and paths. There were forty or fifty members of the group present, all men of course, gathered in a rustic lodge with woods behind it and various paths.

"You formed groups of four, and as a team you shoot at one target, then move on to another. When I got there, I didn't know anyone, which is usually not a problem for me, but I suddenly felt so out of place. It was strange and totally unexpected. I felt I was the only woman in a group of men. My host was the guy I rented office space from. At the time, I had no inkling I would ever become Ellen. Eleanor will swear I'm lying, but on a conscious level . . . I dreamed about it but never thought I had a chance. I remember trying to act in such a way that these guys wouldn't think I was feminine or effeminate—because women are not 'effeminate.'

"At the time I had two different trainers and was trying to bulk up like a man, to be more manly. But simultaneously I was losing a lot of weight, partly for cholesterol, but also to have a feminine shape. It was like I was two twins fighting each other: instead of a devil and an angel, I had a woman on one shoulder, a man on the other, duking it out."

1941: The Haskell parents four years into their marriage
in Fayetteville, North Carolina.

1948: Chevey at three years old in the backyard of the Haskell home on Pocahontas Avenue in Richmond, Virginia.

1948: Chevey, age three, and Molly, age eight, in the garden of the house on Pocahontas Avenue.

1950: Chevey in full cowboy regalia at the Haskells' home in the country outside Richmond.

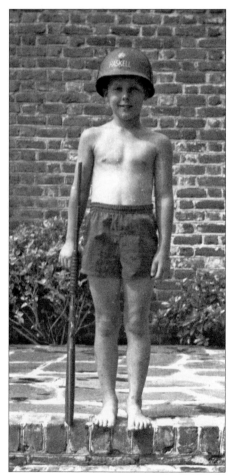

1950: Chevey at age five with rifle and helmet.

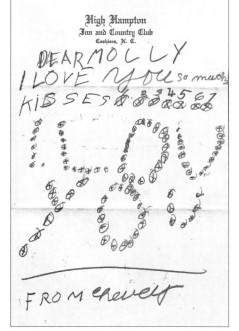

1952: A letter from eight-year-old Chevey at High Hampton, a resort in the mountains of North Carolina, to Molly, thirteen, at nearby Camp Glenlaurel.

1953: Another letter to Molly from Chevey at High Hampton.

1958: Mrs. Haskell (forty-nine) with her son, Chevey (thirteen),
at a debutante ball.

June 1968: Molly and Chevey
at his wedding to Beth in
Richmond. Molly was
a bridesmaid.

Winter 1971: Chevey at
twenty-six years old outside his
farmhouse in Albemarle
County, Virginia.

1992: Chevey and Molly at The Tuckahoe Apartments,
where their mother lived out her final years.

2011: Ellen after she ran
the Tough Mudder
obstacle course.

2011: Ellen on a sailboat off the coast of Key West.

CHAPTER SEVEN

A Tale of Two Wives

*I*t is now March of 2006, and the transition will begin in a month or so. I talk to Eleanor on the phone, ask her how the children are doing. She says they're having a rough time accepting the double whammy of divorce and John's transsexualism.

"They've been very gracious, all things considered, but their first loyalty is to me, and they see how I suffer. I think it's been harder on Adam. His own father was never in his life; John was the man he bonded with, the man he called his dad."

I talk to Beth on the phone as well, and we agree we're both in mourning for "Chiv," his childhood nickname.

I'm so lucky to have these two as friends and in-laws. ("Thanks for being a guy long enough to give me two great sisters-in-law," I tell my brother.) They were also friends with each other, though Chevey's decision has inevitably caused some strain in the relationship. By the time Chevey married Eleanor he was convinced he could suppress the urge indefinitely. He did tell her about it, but even then (the early eighties, about a year after they'd started dating) the whole phenomenon was shrouded in mystery. Now, when we have more knowledge of how set and inalterable these urges are, such a confession would raise red flags; but at the time Eleanor believed, or chose to believe, that he could successfully control it.

"I was very good at hiding it," Chevey says. "Partly this was for my own personal security, but also out of deference to Eleanor. Before we married, I'd told her I had this problem, but I didn't want to remind her of it. This went on for years. Because of it, Eleanor didn't realize the stress. By 2005, I was unraveling on the inside, but it backfired on me. When I finally told her I couldn't suppress it anymore, she was both enraged and outraged: 'Why can't you just carry on as you are?' she asked, over and over. 'You've been doing fine!' I was too good an actor."

They have different versions of this critical juncture. Eleanor insists that he didn't tell her the full story, and if she'd known what transsexualism was, she wouldn't have married him. And yet . . . I want to ask, but I don't: Wasn't there wishful thinking on your part, too? If you'd really wanted to know (Eleanor, intellectually curious and voracious reader), wouldn't you have researched it? And would you now prefer not to have had the marriage at all, and the twenty wonderful years you had together?

Who, in love, doesn't enter marriage in a cloud of irrational hope, blithely ignoring all warning signs? The alcoholic who promises to give up drinking; the philanderer whose love for you will keep him faithful. Chevey with his promise to give up his transsexual dream; Eleanor with her willing suspension of disbelief. And both of them ignoring important differences, like the depth of her commitment to religion and her church. In order for them to get married, Chevey, a nonchurchgoer, had promised the minister he would attend "occasionally."

As time went on, the impasse hardened. When I asked about the divorce, Chevey showed a trace of bitterness. "I spent weeks developing different plans, ways of giving her half of the joint property and half of my net earnings for the rest of her life. She never responded. She hired a lawyer who went on the attack. I'd worked with her for years, taken care of her mother's finances, and suddenly she didn't trust me."

"Why hasn't that poisoned your feelings for Eleanor?" I ask.

"First, because I was the cause of all this; I brought it all on, whether I wanted to or not. Second, it's very rare to find somebody you're that compatible with, and when you do, you want to hold on to them with both hands and make it work. I think in that way transsexuals are optimistic—they want to be accepted and continue to be close to their kids, or spouses. They might think, 'If I do everything right I can salvage this.' You just don't want to lose a person you're so close to.

To me, the ins and outs of marriage and divorce are endlessly fascinating; so much is unknowable. In a dream, Chevey tells me that Andrew's been having an affair for eight years, and I'm devastated. I rant and rave, saying, "Why didn't you tell me? I'd have gotten a divorce." And I wonder if I can unlove him retroactively.

Chevey's told me he never strayed during his marriage. But in a sense, he *has*—his mistress has been his other self.

Chevey couldn't understand the obduracy of Eleanor's attitude; she couldn't understand his lack of empathy for her. To her, he didn't seem to show anguish or remorse.

"If you're going to be a woman, you'd better start showing your feelings," she said.

This I can believe, as Chevey, perhaps during the time of our father's illness, had become an expert in hiding his feelings. His coolness fooled people, even those closest to him.

I could see both sides: the life and married self that Eleanor had constructed lay in shambles, but he had done so much for her and was now entitled to do something for himself. One of the things she complained about was the name he'd selected. But of course, as he told me, he'd chosen it long ago (in the 1970s). The name, like the imagined face, the long blond hair, the willowy figure, belonged to the woman that, in his fantasy life, he already was.

I wonder if perhaps the name was part of what drew him to Eleanor in the first place. Lesser details have sparked elective affinities, and the unconscious hears its own song. For instance, the two women he married, Eleanor and Beth, were exceptionally strong and smart, women who needed plenty of mental legroom. They were also straightforward to the point of bluntness, with nothing of the coquette. Without being dominating, they were dominant types, and their masculine side (which I recognized, *"mon semblable, ma soeur!"*) would fit smoothly and frictionlessly with Chevey's feminine side. Eleanor might not admit it, but something in her was drawn to Chevey precisely because of this pliancy, his openness, his not being threatened by her strength. At one point Andrew and I were talking about the nature of Chevey's two marriages (Andrew being as crazy about both women as I was). When I proposed that Chevey wasn't threatened by their strength, Andrew countered, "They weren't threatened by *his* strength!"

Chevey and Beth's relationship was different. They had known each other, almost presexually, since the age of twelve or fourteen, had gone together and clung to each other as if for survival (it was the period of my father's illness), had lived on a little island of their own.

"It was ghastly," she tells me on the phone. "He had been my soul mate all those years, since we were about fourteen. It shook my world for a long time. My first reaction was to worry about Pete, who was then sixteen months old. How would it affect his life? Then the pain Chiv was in. Then fear—I was so dependent on him, he handled all my business. I had no good friends. He and I really were a world unto ourselves; we talked about *everything*."

"Did you see a therapist?"

"No, Chiv was my therapist."

"How did you manage it?"

"I've had some years to get used to it. But right away, I knew I didn't want to lose him as a friend."

He left her, originally to make the transition, but then found he couldn't. He was living at The Argonaut Company and the extraordinary Beth actually went with him to help him buy clothes.

"We'd go as if we were buying for her," Chevey tells me. "We'd both go into the dressing room, but I'd be the one to try them on. I actually accumulated a nice little wardrobe. Then a funny thing happened. Once I had this wardrobe in a separate closet, I could lock it, and I stopped dressing up. Once I was living alone, I remember going months without feeling the need. I didn't need the connection anymore. I don't know if I actually walked or acted differently, but I just felt freer to think of myself that way."

One day we're discussing the past. It's 2006, I'm still forbidden to write, and Chevey tells me about a near miss that occurred when we had moved back to Richmond. It was night or late evening; I was downstairs and the phone rang. Chevey picked it up and came down to get me, forgetting he'd painted his toenails. As I followed him up the steps, he was in a fit of anxiety lest I should notice his feet, which of course, absorbed in my own adolescent world, I didn't!

Chevey describes a liminal state, the confusion that continued to seep in all during his adolescence and young manhood. "There are moments when you are *ju-u-u-ust* drifting off to sleep, you're no longer conscious but you're not really in sleep yet, where I would have these extremely strong feelings of being a woman. Most nights that probably happened and I didn't know it, but once in a while I'd be feeling it and there would be a noise or something would happen to wake me up and

I could still feel it. But after I gave up the idea of trying to change sex, I swore I wouldn't do it; I said this is insane."

I ask him what he was doing—thinking and feeling—during that period from 1974 until the early eighties when he met Eleanor. I know he went out, since Andrew and I once spent a weekend with him and a sexy young woman who was clearly crazy about him.

"Oh, Nancy," he says. "I actually wasn't dating. I had just left a wonderful marriage and wasn't interested in marrying again. I was simply trying to be normal and hoping my attraction to women would take over. It was Nancy who came after me. She was very persistent, very strong—I seem to have a history of strong women—and she wouldn't take no for an answer. We had great sex, but I had to end it. I didn't want anything permanent and she did.

"And that's how I felt right up to the time I met Eleanor and fell in love. After roughly a year dating her, I told her about the feelings I'd had for years. She and I have different recollections of what I said. Sometimes she dwells on the differences but I keep telling her, 'It doesn't really matter. What we said is irrelevant, because I promised you I would never do anything about it and I've broken that promise.' She thinks that I said that it was over—that I didn't have those feelings anymore. And I think now, I don't know how I could possibly have said that. I mean, the feelings are not something you can get rid of. I might have said I could suppress it. While I can't remember the words, I can't imagine—unless I was drunk—that I could have said that. It's just so counter to everything you feel. Again, it doesn't matter. But she was aware of course all along and every once in a while something would happen or a subject would come up that would create a mildly uneasy feeling between us. I'll make up an example. I don't recall this happening but it must've at some point. There would be a news item, say, about transsexuals. Well, she's sitting there thinking and I'm sitting there thinking but we don't say anything. So things like that would happen. It was something that was never very far away, but at the same time, I never did anything that she could see or sense. I couldn't help the way I felt. I could suppress it. But I couldn't erase it.

"It's like acting as if you don't have a headache. [Once again the "you" instead of the "I."] If you're good at it, you can walk into a room and be pleasant and no one knows that you have a splitting headache. But that doesn't make it go away. And sooner or later you're going to have to deal with that headache. You can only go on so long. And over the course of the years it just gets to the point where it's tearing you up inside. Now on the outside of course you're fighting very hard, just like walking into a party when you have a headache, trying not to show it. I remember once Eleanor said, 'You know, you got this far in life, why couldn't you just go the rest of your life?' And I felt that if I knew it was only three more years, say, perhaps I could've done that. But it also showed me that she doesn't realize, after all she's read about it, how intense, how overpowering, the feeling is.

"And admittedly, from a selfish point of view, you think, I have given the major part of my life to working hard so that you and the kids have a great life. I've helped you raise them, they are all launched now and all that. I think it's time that I do something for myself. And I think that everyone male and female may feel that way. Mine is obviously much more drastic, so that argument kind of falls flat. It's not like I always wanted a sports car so now that all the kids are through college I can go out and buy myself a sports car or a boat.

"Divorce is a closer analogy. One person has been wanting to. But they stay together for the kids, which is not necessarily the best thing. That's the same kind of thing, but I don't pretend for a moment that this is on the same level. But . . ."

"The need is much stronger?"

"The need is a whole lot stronger. Exactly. And the fallout is worse. You can't compare the two. It's something else. But you know, not trying to be melodramatic, but if somebody does something that hurts you, in time the pain eases and you sort of forget about it and maybe you forgive them and you go on. But if you hurt someone else, that stays with you until you die. You can't ever get away from that. And the pain doesn't lessen that much. And there have been so many times when I was thinking about Eleanor and I would just start crying. You think what you've done to somebody. It's like, well, I don't know. There is no other good analogy, except that I've always wondered what it would be like to accidentally kill somebody you love. You're driving, you drop a cigarette in your lap, and the person next to you is killed and you are alive. Same type of thing. I just can't imagine what that would be like for the rest of your life. You would rather have someone cripple *you* because you can forgive them. But if you do it to someone else . . . and I've done that twice. Only two promises I can recollect breaking."

"What was the first?

"Beth."

For all his obvious empathy, there's another side, almost its opposite. From the accounts I've read, transsexuals, for all their sensitivity, can, and perhaps *must*, have a special blind spot when it comes to the reactions of those closest to them. They feel they are "the same person inside," and *they* still love their partners. And because they're finally fulfilling their lifelong dream, goes their reasoning, the people who love them *must* be happy for them.

Eleanor describes the moment of the fatal announcement. It was April of 2005, they were sitting in the sunroom, and Chevey said he'd decided to have surgery. Since he'd just come back from his internist, she was alarmed and asked what was wrong. When he told her he had decided to become a woman, she broke down completely. But to make matters worse, Barbara was marrying in May.

"I asked him if he couldn't have waited until after the wedding to tell me, and he just looked surprised, as if he'd never thought about it."

The plan would have to be kept secret. She couldn't tell Adam or Barbara, who loved Chevey and thought the two of them were happily married. Eleanor would have to go through the whole affair with a happy mother-of-the-bride smile on her face.

"I can see now," Eleanor says, "that he was just so wrapped up in the euphoria of finally being able to realize his dream, he couldn't think about the feelings of others at that moment."

It's as if transsexuals have to wear blinders because they must devote all their mental and emotional energy to the frightening and consuming job ahead, and simply can't allow their feelings of guilt and obligation (obviously strong in Chevey's case) to stop them.

I'm having trouble understanding this until I'm struck by an analogy: the autobiographical writer. We live also in a state of almost willed and necessary denial as to how our work will be received by those close to us. Otherwise we'd be paralyzed by inhibitions. Proust understood that the writer is not so much a person who writes as a person *made* by writing—it's something to which we surrender—as Chevey is being made, or remade, by his femaleness. It's a terrible trade-off. What gives us our deepest feeling of value often involves treading on the sensitivities of others.

When I wrote a book about Andrew's mysterious illness (the illness was in 1984, the book came out in 1991), Mother and Chevey both came into it, but not, I was sure, in any way that could offend. How could I have been so obtuse? Mother was furious and deeply wounded. She didn't say anything at the time, but much later, one evening when she'd had three or four scotches, she sat down and wrote out a list, three pages, single-spaced, of all the "errors" she'd found. These were but a cover for what I grew to feel were deeper wounds. Still, the surface attacks were bad enough; when I read this scorching list of indictments I could hardly breathe.

When she died in 1998, we had a small service, then family and friends came over to her apartment. Afterward, Chevey, Eleanor, Andrew, and I went out for dinner. We took Mother's wallet, letting her pay for it (and surely chastise us from the Other Side for choosing such an expensive restaurant). We had some wine, were feeling very close and mellow, sad and happy, when I mentioned I might write a memoir about Mother. Suddenly Chevey, who I'd never even seen really angry before, exploded. "You just can't do it," he said, concluding, "Suppose you got raped in New York and I wrote about it!"

I was stunned. Tears came to my eyes. Andrew got furious at Chevey on my behalf. We all finally calmed down. We loved and needed each other too much to let this interfere. But it stayed with me and haunted me.

Afterward, I relayed his words about rape to a psychiatrist friend in New York. "He felt violated by your book," he said. Of course! And he felt violated on Mother's behalf. This was what prompted the vehemence of that first injunction, when he came to New York in 2005 and told Andrew and me of his plans: "You have to promise you won't write about this."

But as I thought about it now, and took notes and notes, it seemed I needed to *write* about it as he needed to *do* it.

He was about to take a radical swerve that would have not only a huge impact on his life, but a sizeable one on mine as well. I would be losing my brother without any concrete idea as to what sort of human being would replace him. Answers and explanations were in short supply: I still had no real understanding of the urge that might help me accept it, and no way of talking about it to others. If he felt driven to make his life right by becoming a woman, I was no less driven to seek meaning through words—the "vital impulse to order," as James Olney described the autobiographical urge—and the drive to create was no more a question of conventional "happiness" than transsexualism was.

At least some questions will soon be answered. In April the heroic Eleanor will accompany Chevey for the eleven-hour operation by Dr. Ousterhout, and six months later, there will be a follow-up surgery. Ousterhout, the pioneer in the field, grew interested in facial reconstruction from extensive work as a dental surgeon. I look him up on the Internet; the descriptions are hair-raising. "Scalp advancement surgery," which shortens the distance between eyebrows and hairline, is done, under general anesthesia, with an incision made following the natural hairline. Then there's forehead contouring, also done with anesthesia and incision.

These are but two of an assortment of Frankensteinian improvements on the Web site's menu. There's also the brow lift, eyelid lift, etc. (Now I'm seeing Peter Boyle in the Mel Brooks film, his stitches showing.) When this surgery heals, in about six months, there will be a follow-up surgery to correct the asymmetry of the first: a complete circle can't be cut, as it would sever the nerves and arteries. Beth will accompany Chevey to California for this second and final step of facial reconstruction. The genital surgery will come six months or a year after this.

Chevey and Eleanor go out and I wait by the phone. And wait, with Andrew at my side. Finally Eleanor calls. The operation lasted twelve hours. It went well enough, but he's sore, bandaged, nauseated, and the biggest problem is with the nose, his deviated septum. Eleanor slept in the room with him and is wiped out.

"The doctors are calling him Ellen," she tells me, "so now I have to. The rest of you can wait until the official coming out in May." I can hear her anguish. It's almost as if she didn't believe it would happen right up to the moment of surgery.

"Worst of all was the moment, just before he went into surgery, when we had to remove our wedding rings. We were both in tears."

Though relieved the surgery went well, she can barely speak, so great is her exhaustion and misery. There's a special recovery annex ("cocoon") they share with other transsexuals. It's run by a nurse connected with the doctor, and they have a little basement apartment with separate sleeping facilities, a kitchen, and windows opening onto a garden. Various inmates—bandaged patients and their partners—move around the home, like shadows in a Dantean sexual limbo.

"He looks better than you'd expect," Eleanor says. "There's some pain and nausea, but that's minor compared to the problems with the nose. It's so full of packing—to hold the shape—that he has to breathe through his mouth. Sometimes he wakes up in the night with phlegm in his throat and feels like he's choking. It's frightening. And of course eating is a chore."

I feel so bad for her, or for both "hers." "I wish you had let me go instead of you," I say.

"No, I had to go. It's important for me to see every detail, see how scary and serious it is. Being in on it all, it's a way of letting go.

"Also, I felt it was the least I could do. He's been a wonderful husband, so good to everyone in my family, and that wasn't always easy. He's given so much of himself, treating my children as if they were his own, taking them on trips. Out of decency and respect, I had to support him."

Back in Richmond after Surgery I, Ellen stays with Eleanor for a week and on May 11 leaves for Pine Mountain, and then the announcement goes out. There's a basic letter, varied according to whether business or personal, relative or acquaintance. Chevey worked on it for days, consulting with Beth and me, but it's entirely his:

Dear ＿＿＿＿＿＿＿＿,

    I have something important to tell you that you will find difficult to believe, but I assure you that it is quite true. I wish I could be with you to tell you this in person, but I have a number of people that I need to inform at the same time, so unfortunately a letter is the only way.

    My entire life I have been struggling with what is now referred to as a "gender identity disorder." This means that I have continually been tormented by intense feelings that I should have been born female instead of male. I decided a year ago that it was no longer possible to suppress this need. After extensive therapy, I am now in the process of becoming a woman and am at the stage where I am required by my doctors to live full time in my new identity. Therefore, I am now Ellen Hampton and am no longer Chevey Haskell.

    I wouldn't be doing this if the anguish weren't lifelong, overwhelming, and debilitating. While countless others have taken this step, I realize this is a matter that few people know much about. I hope you will try to be understanding.

Sincerely,
Ellen

CHAPTER EIGHT

The Sculptor of Human Faces

It's a lot of work for a woman to look good, but it's a thousand times more work for a man to look good as a woman.

—Ellen Hampton

*N*othing happens! Silence. I'm waiting for the sky to fall and there's not a single call. Or e-mail. A relief, but also decidedly odd. I've kept the secret to myself for seven whole months, but on the red-letter day, I've made a date (with Ellen's permission) to see Jeanne, my oldest friend from Richmond. We go back to childhood. Our lives were always diverging—she majored in math, I in English; in our first election, she voted for Nixon, I for Kennedy; and as I tried to carve out a path in the arts, she went to work for IBM and then had four children. But we have remained as close as sisters.

I hadn't shed a tear, but now I wept. It was both a relief and an ordeal, for it made it all more real and irreversible. Jeanne was profoundly accepting, worrying only about Chevey's health and happiness, and my own. She represented all that was warm and unconditionally loving in my background, but also she was here, in New York, like me. Not representative of the world of my upbringing, or the world at large, either.

At home, I wait for repercussions, cousins calling, angry, outraged, or simply wanting details. Nothing! Again a deafening silence that is a relief but also unsettling. The one person who eventually calls is my adored cousin Preston. A year and a half older than I, an entrepreneur in Jacksonville with an expansive and generous personality, he's shocked but completely sympathetic. No doubt the others simply don't know what to say. Chevey, or rather Ellen, gets letters from some of them as well as business acquaintances and is heartened.

I tell a few more people: Betty, a former New York roommate and television reporter, is the only one of my New York friends who knew him and, having done stories on the subject, is both knowledgeable and sympathetic. Betty asks if she can call Ellen, and I readily agree. She does and reports back to me that they had a wonderful conversation, that she sounds remarkably grounded and realistic. Take notes! says Betty. And of course I do, though I am still pledged to silence as far as writing a book.

Meanwhile, what else can I do but write in my journal, as I have always done, recording everything from bowel movements and migraines to thoughts on films, books, news items. Words flow, not as from a "writer," giving shape and form to grief, but simply from a person trying to navigate the rising waters with a raft of words—trying to gain some form of control. Even fractured syntax and spontaneous outpourings round out the present with a period, turn it into the past, and give one the illusion of moving forward. Yet I know from experience that the transformation of thoughts into form, of perceptions into patterns (not to mention gratification of the ego), comes only by writing for publication, gaining mastery of the narration. My need is to explain Chevey not just to myself but to those out of earshot of my journal, and especially to my mother and father, in some mystical hope of reconciling them and "making it right."

And what—for I can't stop thinking about it—would our parents' reactions have been? The response of my father, a gentleman in both senses of the word but a hard-core conservative, is simply impossible to imagine. Would he have preferred that Chevey just disappear into a new sex and a faraway location, as he'd planned to do at one time? I think of some of the Lear-like scenes in Ovid when parents confront a loved one transformed. In one of the cruelest, the father of Io finds his daughter turned into a cow. All she can do is moo, a sound that so frightens her, she can't bear the sound of her own voice. (One of the harshest fates Ovid provides for his transfigured creatures is the loss of the human voice, and Chevey is losing his beautiful baritone to something that wavers between a tenuous contralto and what he calls a Tiny Tim falsetto.) Perhaps our father would have reacted like Io's, who cried out the bone-chilling words "Lost, you were less a grief than you are, found!"

Would Mother have felt similarly? It's painful to think of her reaction but impossible not to speculate. The sense of her grief and horror is as palpable as if she were alive. I imagine utter devastation, shock, revulsion, a mortification that goes beyond simple shame or embarrassment. Possibly even a stroke or heart attack, or deep depression. But I'm simply imagining her as a woman of her time and place, reacting in a generic way and on a single occasion. What part would love and the passage of time have played? For if her taking the news with equanimity is inconceivable, neither can I imagine our mother never wanting to see her adored child again. Mother love, mysteriously resilient, is capable of weathering an almost infinite number of shocks to the system. Such maternal acceptance seems to have been granted to other transsexuals, so why not ours? And if I concede such largeness of spirit to Mother, should I deprive our father of a similar capacity to rise to the occasion? Mightn't love burn through his own crusts of tradition and resistance?

My own impulse to blow the lid off privacy is undoubtedly a reaction to the straitjacket of a culture, a family, of silence and discretion.

Mine was not the South of Eudora Welty or William Faulkner, of sittin'-on-the-porch and storytelling and confabulating, of secrets passed around, but the South of retreat from display, stoical reserve, secretiveness, and silence. Except when liquor loosened tongues and gossip turned ugly.

Even as a child I was a nonstop talker and questioner, often driving my poor parents crazy. So naturally I fled this buttoned-up world for New York City, magnet for blabbermouths, and eventually found sanctuary at the *Village Voice*, the Wild West of cultural journalism. There I wrote about plays, then movies, and—my own form of "liberation"—was drawn to exploring sexual subtexts.

Meanwhile, Ellen is at Pine Mountain, in abject misery. It's May, then June, of 2006, and she's still very sore, her nose hurts all the time, she has no sense of smell and no desire to eat. Moreover, it's as if she's under house arrest. An inveterate walker, she barely steps outside her apartment, is uncomfortable walking around the complex, and waits until dark to take her garbage to the bin. Constantly terrified of exposure, when she goes into town for groceries, she first has to spend hours on hair, makeup, and dress, and once in the store, buys only items already wrapped and priced, which she can then pay for at the automatic checkout.

When we talk—often, as I'm trying to keep her spirits up—her voice remains the same, which allows me to continue to think of her as Chevey. Voice surgery as it's now practiced is worse than useless, and those transsexuals who've undergone the procedure have cautioned against it. The hormones don't affect the voice, so the only real way to transform that most important signifier is speech therapy. It's hard, arduous, and Ellen is not yet up to it. Another setback: They told her, as she was going in for the tracheal shave, that one side effect could be a permanent lowering of the voice. Alas, this seems to have happened;

as reflected in the computer diagram she uses for speech therapy, she can no longer reach her highest register—the "Tiny Tim" falsetto she used in practice before the surgery.

On a recent trip to town, she uses the ladies' room for the first time (one obstacle met) and, also for the first time, goes to the bank. Every visit she's on tenterhooks, trying to act natural. They know, she's sure. But they act normal. The desire to "pass," to be accepted as female, is a longing weighted with existential dread.

"I always had this kind of waking nightmare," she tells me. "In this scenario I'm walking down the sidewalk at a local shopping center as a woman with her little daughter passes me, going in the opposite direction. And as I walk by, the little girl turns to her mom and says, 'Mommy, why is that man dressed up like a woman?' For years before I transitioned, this was always the fear. When even little children 'read' you—which they sometimes do better than adults."

The movie *Transamerica* has recently come out. Felicity Huffman is terrific as a man in her year of presenting as a woman—awkward but convincing, and with a desperate need for reassurance. I understand the agonizing scene when her character is "read." She's at a diner somewhere midcountry (transsexuals in movies never stay put in like-minded communities, nor do they ever *fly* over flyover country but on some pretext must invariably plow through indigenous hives of bigotry). She's ordering lunch and in the next booth are a mother and daughter. The little girl peers over the top of her seat and, after a good stare, turns and asks her mother, "Is that a man or a woman?" whereupon a traumatized Huffman rushes to the pay phone and tearfully calls her therapist.

This is a lost year, we agree, but what about when she's out and about? I ask what might happen if she "meets someone." And the possibility of danger. I'll always be up front about it, she says. If a man seems interested, I'll tell him. This I entirely approve of and is totally in character, my honorable and "straight" brother now sister. Despite Hilary Swank's virtuoso performance as Teena Brandon/Brandon Teena in *Boys Don't Cry*, I hated the duplicity. Yes, the yahoos were uptight and murderous, but she in some sense invited the violence by taunting their manhood, pulling the wool over their eyes, and acting in bad faith. The fact is that a large number of transsexuals are murdered every year by those who feel duped and threatened.

In June Andrew and I attend a wedding in Dallas. My friend Jeanne's second son, Will, is marrying the enchanting Heather, whom he met at Duke. We're all going to stay at the Four Seasons, where the wedding and reception will take place, the chance for a luxury getaway and reunion with friends. It's a Jewish wedding, something my Richmond friends have never seen, and I love the sight of Jeanne, red-faced and laughing aloft on the huppah, and even more the wide-eyed looks on the Richmonders' faces. At the same time, I'm on guard, alert to any meaningful exchange of glances, signs of being in the know. It seems pretty clear that the disclosure to intimates on May 11 hasn't gotten out. I'm amazed and speculate it has something to do with my family's self-protective wall of silence. Apparently gossip this toxic travels slowly in Richmond.

Also in attendance are a couple, Patricia and Jim, old friends of Chevey and Beth's, and for the last twenty years, friends of Eleanor's as well. I've been chatting with them (as briefly as possible) all weekend, deflecting questions about Chevey and Eleanor, but suddenly I feel I can't maintain the fiction any longer. I call Ellen on my cell and suggest I tell them. She's delighted (easier for me than for her!) but worries about how difficult it will be for me. It is, yet it's something I can do for her and also test the waters. Still baffled that no one has found out (and it's quite clear they haven't), I ask them to sit down and brace themselves, while I go through the whole story. They're in utter shock, but grateful and concerned, and I'm relieved. Sort of. I report to Ellen.

Will you call him "sister," Eleanor asks. I say I don't think so, can't quite. She agrees, a sister is someone you grew up with as a sister. Yes, but then, marriage is something that was entered into by a man and a woman and has now come to encompass gay unions.

Ellen does discuss hair, as Beth had feared, but not ad nauseam, considering how crucial a role it plays. She can't control it, wants to keep her own so she can eventually get rid of the wig. We discuss different kinds of hair dryers and gel. She tells me that when she looks in the mirror, she sometimes sees Mother and sometimes me. Then she helps me with computer questions.

July 24, 2006. Eleanor's first glimpse. Ellen will come to visit next week, and Eleanor will see her for the first time in full female regalia. Eleanor wants to do it, though she isn't really ready, so she can realize that it's truly "over" and get on with her life. Otherwise there's always some hope in the back of her mind, or even just the image of him as he was, which she'll want to keep. When dying loved ones shrink and decay, we hope we can retain the image of them as they were, but here it's the opposite: we must try to forget.

Then The Visit occurs and Eleanor calls, disobeying the gag order. She told Ellen she refused to keep silent, was going to tell me and her children her impressions. To her horror and against all expectation, she burst into tears. It was an enormous shock. First, Ellen did resemble Mother. Then, she wore jeans and a tunic-type top, beads and earrings, and fingernail polish. That doesn't sound like Mother, but Chevey was so much more like Mother than I was, in both temperament (she always said so) and looks. He and Mother had the same narrow face, blue eyes (his aqua-blue, hers blue-gray), regular, aquiline features as opposed to my rounder ones. Mother had been a beauty. What would Chevey be?

The two worst features, says Eleanor, were the hands, which are male and ropey, and the wig—too much hair for her thin face.

When I get off the phone I feel equally shocked and disturbed, as if I've seen her myself. It's real to me for the first time. I've been living in a fool's paradise. Now I'll have to think about how she looks, what she wears, the sum total of the all-important presentation. As a man he didn't have to have "taste," just wear slacks and a blazer, or suit and tie.

I begin having dreams about my mother. She's back among us; we have buried her alive.

I tell Andrew my fears. We begin talking of his brother, George, three years younger, the daredevil to Andrew's cautious old-man-before-his-time. They loved each other, but Andrew, their mother's favorite, felt that he'd never shown George his love, never paid enough attention.

"If I could have my brother back, alive, I'd take him on any terms," Andrew says. "Male or female!"

With trepidation, a little prepared speech, and a request for secrecy, Eleanor tells her church group. Up till now she's just told them he and she are separated, and she feels hypocritical when the solicitous friends keep asking if there's any chance they'll get back together.

I understand her chagrin: as uncomfortable as we are discussing the subject, we're more distressed by our deception and bad faith in keeping silent.

Andrew and I are having dinner at the home of Billy and Annette Cobbs, old friends of ours and of my cousin Preston's. Preston has told

Billy the news, and Billy, a charming, good ole Alabama boy, is wild with amazement and shock. And a subversive streak. "What will Suzanne think?" he asks with a mischievous smile when I arrive, referring to a mutual friend and distant relative, a Belle of the Confederacy turned New York doyenne to whom I'm distantly related. Billy imagines the horror of gene-proud cousins, the look on their faces. "Suzanne's the last person I care about," I say honestly, with some annoyance. "She'll probably find she was mistaken about the family connection!"

While enjoying the food and good cheer of another of Annette's gastronomic feats, I'm seated across from a woman, a writer, I've come to know and admire in recent years. We start talking about our pasts, as one does in a deepening relationship, and she tells the extraordinary story of how the death of a brother shaped her life. She was only three, he a few years older, and the family was shattered. In reaction to the tragedy, she became the child who would make it up to her parents, would do everything he would have done, excel in everything. She did, even dressing as a boy, and it explains her astonishing work ethic and achievement, but imagine the lifetime pressure of trying to meet some standard of perfection that by its very nature is both vague and unattainable. Then she asks me about siblings and whether I still have any family in Richmond. I mumble something about a brother and quickly change the subject. This is not the time or place to spill the beans, but I inwardly recoil from the evasion.

And if Billy knows, it's time to tell some more of my friends. I'm still in a quandary about going public. Because I am a talker, part of me wants desperately to tell a few more friends, get some reactions, lift the burden. But I dread the questions, hundreds of them, the very ones I'd posed. I want them to know, all at once, without my having to tell them. Ethel had said, "You don't have to tell people." But I do. The idea of keeping it a secret hadn't even occurred to me. As little as I want to talk about it, I'm equally averse to (and possibly incapable of) maintaining a wall of silence. Something in me needs to have it *out there*, to exorcise the secret so it's no longer shameful. And if someone asks me if I have siblings, or even for news of my brother? Am I supposed to lie, or crudely change the subject?

"They may write or say very supportive things," Ethel had said, "but what they're thinking and saying away from you is another matter." I have a blind spot where reactions are concerned, and was taken aback when the title of my first book, *From Reverence to Rape*, created something of a scandal, particularly in my hometown. This denial is what allows me to plunge ahead, ignoring the consequences, yet I can't help but believe that shame and secrecy are harder to bear than exposure and ridicule. One is held prisoner by shame, which simply reinforces the stigma. The way cancer was once unmentionable, or a child's mental disability, or homosexuality—as if their exposure would not only taint the sufferer but reflect on the family as well—so transsexualism now occupies the role of Unspeakable.

I wish it could be suddenly known without my having to do the disclosing. It's not just the endless questions, but how could I ever explain what a wonderful person my brother was? And then, "It's such a juicy tidbit," I tell a friend. "It's too anguished a subject for gossip," she replies.

Another old friend comes to New York and we have lunch. I want to explain why Andrew and I didn't accept her invitation the previous summer, one that would have involved getting a ride from Ellen to the Virginia mountain retreat where my friend was hosting the weekend. After making the disclosure, I confessed I simply couldn't have faced it. She's very quiet, and unlike the other recipients of the information, doesn't question me further. (After all, she's a Virginian.) Is she uncomfortable or simply discreet? I can understand discomfort, even recoil—one is forced to visualize, at least for a moment until repression comes to the rescue, and that visualization makes us uncomfortable.

"Everything will be natural," Chevey had said on that fateful day in October, at the beginning of the transition. "Nothing artificial . . . I don't want to look like Marilyn Monroe, just a normal woman." He intended not to have breast implants and his hair would be his own. But what a lot of other alterations there would be. I get up the nerve to ask him exactly what the facial reconstruction surgery involved.

"First, some things were taken away, but none were added. Unlike cosmetic surgery, this has nothing to do with beauty, or trying to look younger or like a certain person. It's only about subtraction, removing obvious masculine characteristics. The first thing Ousterhout did was pull out a ruler and measure everything. The man's forehead is higher than the woman's, so he shortened the forehead. He takes out part of the skin, pulls the hairline further forward, and raises the eyebrows slightly. [This is all under general anesthetic, of course.] Second, the male forehead protrudes further out relative to the rest of the face (it's less now, but think of Neanderthal man). You can't just saw away part of the forehead, because it would break through to open nasal cavities, so he has to break the forehead into pieces and remake it, putting together the pieces in a way that is less protruding. The result is very subtle, a matter of maybe a millimeter or two. I don't even notice it but he does. It's why he's the best.

"With the nose he changes the angle of the ski slope part, the tip and the width, to give me a smaller, more feminine nose. I think he even made my nostrils smaller.

"Next, in my way of thinking, which may not be the order in which he did it, he shrinks the distance from the top of the upper lip to the nose, which is less in a woman than a man, just like the forehead. That's why if a woman relaxes her mouth so that it's slightly open, you'll see the upper teeth. If a man does the same thing, you see either no teeth or lower teeth. In photographs of women you see the upper teeth but not in those of men.

"Proceeding down the face, there's the jaw. On the male, the chin sticks out a little further than in the female. So he goes in and takes off some of the bone. He can't just sand it down, he has to break it and wire it back together. He uses titanium on some parts of the face, stainless steel on others. He assured me I'd have no trouble getting through airport security. The male jaw is much heavier than the female's. He took bone off the back and sides of the jaw. Then the tracheal shave, which removes the Adam's apple."

I ask why there were no scars.

"Because he's such an expert. He used to sculpt as a hobby, in wood. Eleanor said she could see that in the final result—as if he were carving in wood or ivory. He pioneered by studying all these skulls; there were some two thousand, and he spent days on them.

"It was just so important for me to get it all as perfect as possible. I feel bad for those transsexuals, so many of them, who can't afford it, because the first thing you look at is the face. I was fortunate to have enough savings to do it."

The next round, where she'll be accompanied by Beth and her husband Randy, will correct problems created by the first surgery. So when the skin heals, the second phase of the surgery—only six hours this time—will complete the process. Eleanor's daughter, Barbara, will come down from northern California to see her. She's requested a photograph as preparation—an excellent idea, I think. Ellen, wanting to control the drama of her coming out and get independent reactions from her near and dear, resists such a move, feeling it won't give the whole picture. But that's just the point. A partial revelation, a glimpse. In the privacy of our own reactions. We convince her that it will help us enormously, a kind of interim exposure that will help us get used to her.

Ellen's may be an extreme version, and may, as she says, have nothing to do with aesthetic enhancement (although I think she may be protesting too much), but it's still the next stage in the art and technology of cosmetic surgery. Hers may not fit the category of altruistic or therapeutic, like the war wounds, burns, and birth defects for which it was originally invented. But it's a matter of greater urgency than the whole spectrum of knife-wielding improvements that have gone from being the slightly shameful vice of Park Avenue matrons and movie stars to a massive billion-dollar industry catering to what Alex Kuczynski calls "beauty junkies."

Time was when men and women would pass "naturally" into the age of androgyny, looking more and more like each other as facial muscles drooped, eyes dimmed, gray hair thinned, whiskers sprouted, voices met in the middle, alto-contralto, trousers became the default wardrobe. Now such signs of aging are to be found in a minority, a curious little tribe of stubborn, untransfigured "elderly," who with their canes and walkers toddle among us like harbingers of a mortality we refuse to believe in. Our enchantment with enhancements—from butt reduction to Botox—has a good excuse. Now we live longer and feel healthier; the image we see in the mirror doesn't match our sense of ourselves. And if the here-and-now is all we have—without the consolations of religion, and with no spiritual payoff in leaving the flesh and its mortifications "as God made them"—then who among us can stand alone or stare down the looks-and-youth obsession that dominates our lives and turns every face and body into a work in progress?

Because of Eleanor's strict religious beliefs, Ellen's transformation has been especially troubling.

"Eleanor said one time that God does not make mistakes," Ellen tells me, "implying that it was a sinful thing to transition from a man to a woman. You frequently hear, 'God hates the sin but loves the sinner.' But her comment had to do with not making mistakes and I thought about that a lot, and my opinion then, as now, was suppose you use the analogy of birth defect. Say a boy is born with some kind of spinal injury or malformation that prevents him from walking. He grows up in a wheelchair, and when he's a teenager, or maybe later, medical science has devised a surgery that would correct the problem. Well, first of all, you could say, 'If God doesn't make mistakes, why was this boy born unable to walk?' The usual answer is, 'Well, it's God's purpose.' Maybe God was trying to prepare the boy for some higher purpose? Still, if the possibility of a corrective operation had arisen, you wouldn't think there was something spiritually wrong with him having that operation. So I think, why doesn't that same reasoning apply to me? Why can't I change something that I feel was like a birth defect, something wrong?"

"Maybe," I suggest, "because your 'defect' seems so subjective, people don't yet understand it." Even a visible birth defect like hermaphroditism, having both male and female sex organs, presents a more universally compelling case for surgery.

"But in any event," Ellen continues, "it's not really rational to say that God doesn't make mistakes, because we don't know. Maybe there is a purpose in all of this. So that is my feeling about people who think that it is some sort of sin. Certainly my life has been pretty sedate; I'm not wild and reckless."

Eleanor is a woman whose everyday life revolves around the teachings of the Bible, and who lives her religion. She always said grace before meals, not the formulaic one, but one adapted to each of us and our present situations—e.g., asking God to protect us in our travels, support some upcoming trial, thanking Him for bringing us together. As one who practices foxhole religion—officially a nonbeliever who nevertheless prays to Providence or the Great All-Seeing in emergencies—I was somewhat put off by these personalized expressions of thanksgiving but drew comfort from the generosity of the impulse. I call her, as I need to hear in her own words how this has affected her reaction.

"Everybody has their faith. I feel very strongly that God creates us the way He wants us to be. John was treading on sacred ground, taking over the creative power that only God should have. I couldn't shake my fist in the face of God like he was doing. God had made him a man and given him the strength to be one for sixty-five years. I was afraid in a religious way. And I don't think I'm a religious nut; I'm pretty mainstream, but with strongly held beliefs."

Some of this religious feeling about what is natural and God given, whether explicit or residual, informs the ambivalence toward surgical enhancement that runs through our culture, even as we stand in line to buy Beauty and Youth at the hands of willing doctors. Reviewing a book on the cosmetic surgery industry, Sherwin Nuland calls our current obsession "the culture of inauthenticity." But the word "authenticity" has become a slippery concept indeed in a culture where image usurps reality at every turn, and "reality" shows are as phony as three-dollar bills. The argument is not artifice versus nature but which kinds of authenticity seem acceptable, then natural—which reality is "real"—at any given time. Once brandished by flower children and war resisters as a badge of integrity, a challenge to the hypocrisy of their warmongering elders, "authenticity" has become its opposite, a code-word-as-sales-pitch used by politicians to burnish their flips and flops; a claim made by participants on Facebook and other media Web sites even as they Photoshop their images and biographies.

A Web site called Cloud Girlfriend encourages creating a fantasy profile as the beginning of a beautiful relationship. For anyone born after 1960, many of the distinctions between "true" and "false" (e.g., computer-generated imagery versus film; photographed reality versus photographed "re-creations") are meaningless.

Computerized voices constitute a rather large fraction of daily communication, robots perform increasingly sophisticated tasks: our machines are extensions of ourselves, endowed with human qualities. The line between fact and fiction is constantly debated, constantly crossed, the blurring of boundaries increasingly accepted, as in the hybrid genre latterly defined as "autofiction." Cindy Sherman, in her multiple guises and disguises, never invites us to wonder about the "real" Cindy Sherman but, on the contrary, glories in the profusion and confusion of identities she's able to summon up. Bob Dylan's astonishing metamorphosis from Midwestern Jewish boy to Zeitgeisty troubadour is captured in the film *I'm Not There* by having six different actors play his distinct personae. The doppelganger is the stock-in-trade of writers who are always creating alter egos; how can it not be when they are funneling parts of themselves from the unconscious into the DNA of their protagonists?

People die and a whole other identity comes to the fore, as was the case when Alan Feuer, a *New York Times* reporter, paid homage to a man bearing his name, an aristocrat-impostor who concealed his Jewish immigrant background. He'd gone to England, then become the epitome of the English gentleman, a fixture at New York's Old World society balls. One of the dead man's friends astutely remarks, "I don't like the phrase 'reinvent yourself.' I think what really happened is that when Alan got to England, whatever he found there allowed him to discover who he already was."

"Emerge" is the current preferred description. Old personae, exit stage right: enter new personae with different names and faces. "Is there an end to perpetual becoming?" Richard Ford's Frank Bascombe asks.

But what is transsexualism? Is it an invention or a discovery? In fact, it's both. Feuer's new persona may have been what he considered his authentic self, but it also required enormous invention, fabrication. Most changes don't occur so dramatically or so visibly. Like the changes in a marriage, or from one love object to another. We can no more truly capture that moment of change or its preceding experience of pain or ecstasy or boredom than Proust's Swann, once out of love, could recall the sensation of passionate love for Odette or relive its intensity.

It's why, Proust suggested, novels (and, I would add, movies) provide such pleasure: they accelerate change, give characters a movement, an "arc," endow lives with the climaxes, turning points, and the illusion of meaning we so desperately want. The transsexual, however, contradicts the natural rhythm of change; he's a movie, a music video, an overnight transformation.

A woman writes an op-ed piece about how changing her name turned her, or allowed her to turn herself, into another person. In her book *Nom de Plume*, Carmela Ciuraru cites and analyzes the large number of writers who have pseudonyms. She contrasts the courage of great literary bifurcated beings like George Eliot and Isak Dinesen with the less noble and consequential deceptions of bloggers and their ilk. The latter present alternate selves as if dressing in a Hallowe'en costume when the occasion arises, whereas the writers are more like transvestites (I'd substitute "transsexuals" here) whose "self-presentation is bound up inextricably, profoundly and even painfully with . . . identity. It's the difference between striking a pose and learning to walk."

Ellen has the good fortune to be learning to walk at a time of greater cultural leniency in such matters, but the misfortune to "emerge" at a time when image rules, when youth and beauty are a twenty-four-hour obsession, and the criteria are perhaps more cruelly elitist than they've ever been. Not only that, but the transsexual fails to abide by the gender-fashionable dictum of blurring boundaries or theatricalizing gender. With the female-to-male there might be prejudice or the kind of aversion that greets the "butch" dyke. But with the male-to-female transsexual, there's the attempt at "true" femaleness that can fail so disastrously and publicly.

CHAPTER NINE

He Learns to Walk and Talk Like a Dame

The mystery of the world is the visible, not the invisible.

—Oscar Wilde as quoted by Susan Sontag

*C*hevey wanted Ellen, and Ellen wants Ellen, to be the "best woman I can be." This makes me uncomfortable, as if there were a single criterion for something as vast and multiform as woman. But as I question her, she makes clear she doesn't mean some essentialist concept of *femaleness*, or even goodness. It's not a question of character, but—for safety and her own satisfaction—it's about her persuasiveness as a woman. Her guidelines will be from those periods when, according to her, women looked and dressed like women.

Andrew once made a similar observation about an even earlier time. We were walking along Fifth Avenue after a screening, and everyone we passed (as my mother would have said) "looked like scat," underdressed (possibly because most were now tourists) in some form of sneakers and unisex comfort clothes. He wistfully recalled that in the fifties, he and his army buddies used to come to New York and descend on Midtown just to look at the beautiful girls. Was my generation responsible for the change? We'd shudderingly rejected the Donna Reed small-waisted girly look—one of the few styles that hadn't come back as retrochic. I was sure Ellen wouldn't wear waist cinchers or full skirts, but what period of fashion would she adopt?

Thinking of how this would go down in Richmond made my hair

stand on end. But dealing with it in New York would be no picnic either. I could imagine the gossip, the snickers. Only months before, a friend and I had rolled our eyes and laughed when she told me of a wedding she'd attended where one of the mothers of the bride was a former male, now female, all dolled up, monumental, on the arm of her new male companion. It's the drag aspect that unsettles, the parody of femininity.

One night Andrew and I are having dinner with friends—a therapist, J, and her husband. J tells of walking into her waiting room to greet her next patient, a pre-op male-to-female transsexual, and being taken aback by the sight of the woman, with huge hands and feet, dressed in gloves and hat, everything "matchy-matchy, like a 1950s lady." J's eyes widen in merriment but also distress. As we all laugh, Andrew and I a little uncomfortably, I think perhaps she, too, is surprised at her own momentary shock, distaste, even prejudice. Is it the essential fact of it that bothers her, or the fashion grotesquerie? In other words, is the offense against nature or against style, or can the two be separated?

In some ways, both the flamboyant cross-dresser and the blurred-gender icon are easier to accept than the transsexual. The weirdo, the proudly transgressive performer, and the androgyne, creature of art and imagination—ethereal pansexual icons like David Bowie, Tilda Swinton, Johnny Depp, Patti Smith, Hilary Swank—are as immaterial as Orlando. They allow us to feel we recognize the mixture of male and female "in all of us" at a comfortable distance. They rarely cause a jab in the genitals, a sense of the ground giving way beneath us. These, generally, are what gender progressives mean when they speak approvingly of "challenging stereotypes." Yet it's the transsexual who truly challenges stereotypes—by reaffirming them.

At once ultraradical and ultraconservative, the transsexual is the most paradoxical of creatures: on the outer edge of society in wishing to alter his sex, but conventional, even retrograde, in the ideal of womanhood he embraces, and the yearning to "fit in."

One of the great ironies is that although the transsexual can't be seen apart from the ideology of sexual liberation, with its attendant advances in science and technology, she has proved a thorn in the side of gender liberationists. During the early seventies, transsexuals were labeled "Uncle Toms" by the very women who most rabidly opposed a strict gender dichotomy. At a time when transsexuals already faced huge obstacles, militant feminists denounced butch lesbians on one side and transsexuals on the other for emulating benighted forms of "patriarchy." At a West Coast lesbian conference in Los Angeles in 1973, Robin Morgan gave a notorious speech, demanding that the conference refuse admission to the transsexual lesbian singer Beth Elliott. She proceeded to deliver a jeremiad about the "obscenity of male transvestism" and "men who deliberately *re*-emphasize gender roles, and who parody female oppression and suffering." Making no distinction between the male-to-female transsexual and the occasional drag or heterosexual cross-dresser, she accused them of not having suffered enough to earn the title "woman." After suggesting they might even enjoy being hassled on the street by a man, she concluded, "He dares, he dares to think he understands our pain? No, in our mothers' names and in our own, we must not call him sister."

When the talk was later published in an anthology, Morgan wrote in her introduction, "It was incredible that so many strong angry women should be divided by one smug male in granny glasses and an earth-mother gown."

The feminist theologian Mary Daly labeled transsexuality a "necrophilic invasion" of women's space, and her student Janice G. Raymond took these strands further in her book *The Transsexual Empire:*

The Making of the She-Male (1979), in which she accuses transsexuals of raping women's bodies.

Could it be that the granny glasses and the earth-mother gown (or, in the East Coast version, the club lady with suit and matching gloves) are an offense greater even than the man-made vagina? Or that while we may recoil from the cruelty and unhinged nastiness of Morgan's remarks, some part of us agrees with some part of her argument?

Woman to J. Michael Bailey, author of the inflammatory *The Man Who Would Be Queen*: "When they say they feel like women, how do they know what that feels like?"

I ask Ellen the same question.

"Basically I think you learn enough growing up around women, from lifelong contact with their reading, ideas, conversation, what matters to them. Some people think I am trying to relive parts of my life that I missed. I lived through each phase in my imagination."

If, as Ellen says, it's a thousand times harder for a man to look like a woman, how can all that time and energy spent on appearance not change a person? How can the Ellen obsessed with the outside be the same person as Chevey was inside? I wonder about Jennifer Boylan and Jan Morris: How does it feel to them to feel like women? How do their thoughts and feelings match their outer selves, and how "authentic" do they feel? From photographs, Jennifer, being younger and more typically feminine, seems to have made an attractive-looking female, while Morris by most accounts, before settling into dignified-dowdy, went through a grotesquely awkward wannabe-girl period. At least that's how Nora Ephron saw it. In a witty but unforgiving review of *Conundrum*, Ephron declared that she, too, always wanted to be a girl but felt that she "was born into the wrong body." Lean and boyish, she longed to be "feminine in the worst way—coquettish, submissive . . . dependent, soft-spoken." She was no good at being a girl, she wrote, but "not half bad at being a woman," whereas by contrast, "Jan Morris is perfectly awful at being a woman; what she has become instead is exactly what James Morris wanted to become those many years ago. A girl. And worse, a forty-seven-year-old girl. And worst of all, a forty-seven-year-old *Cosmopolitan* girl."

While bowing to *Conundrum* as a pioneering masterpiece, Boylan, who cites Ephron in her memoir, has to concede that there is an adolescent tone to much of what she and her fellow transsexuals do. This is because they who are "going through transition resemble nothing so much as gawky, wonder-struck teenagers, amazed and perplexed by their bodies, startled by an awareness of themselves as men or women, as if they have invented the whole business single-handedly then and there. There is nothing as annoying as someone for whom the world is new. At least to those for whom the world is old."

Boylan even admits that time and again she herself had fallen giddily and helplessly into this same trap . . . wearing toenail polish, applying makeup on Sundays, reading fashion magazines, dieting crazily. All of which gets at what annoys many women: the emphasis on clothes and makeup by women who've never had a menstrual cycle, never given birth; the sense that they're wallowing in the "good parts," the "trappings" of womanhood, without having endured the specifically female ordeals.

On the other hand, Boylan suggests, transsexuals are treated to inordinate scrutiny and criticized for things many other women do. In the early days, people would look at her and conclude she didn't know what she was doing—which in effect she didn't. But "plenty of other women—including forty-three-year-olds—behave in ways much more embarrassing than I did. Women *born* women are given the right to define womanhood on their own terms." Nevertheless, "a transsexual who hopes to build a life around high heels and sponge cake is in for something of a disappointment."

A friend tells me an anecdote. She was in a shop on Madison Avenue and saw a woman, clearly a transsexual, trying on a dress. She was struck by the way she gazed at herself in the mirror, the way she posed, and the obvious pleasure she took from it. "Women never think they're that beautiful," she said.

Nor do all transsexuals, incidentally. Renée Richards has candidly acknowledged her regrets, none of which involve a wish to go back in time and become a man again. There's the pain it caused others—the traumatized son, the lost wife. There's the arduousness of the process, at the end of which she still didn't feel like an authentic, biological woman. And finally her disappointingly brief shelf life as a sexually desirable woman. "I had a very full sexual life," she has said, "both as a man and in the first few years as a woman. [But] an unmarried woman at sixty-four is a lot different than an unmarried man of sixty-four."

Meanwhile, during the year of presenting and the next one, the sixty-one-year-old Ellen will have more lessons in comportment, dress, makeup, and, unhappily and into the foreseeable future, electrolysis. Patty, her electrologist, works with over a hundred transsexuals and, according to Ellen, "knows more about 'Ts' than anyone I've ever known, including therapists and surgeons."

"Facial hair is where the female-to-male has a big advantage over the male-to-female," Ellen explains. "A woman can take testosterone and grow a beard, even deepen her voice. But when a man takes estrogen, his facial hair doesn't stop growing. He has to have electrolysis for years, and that's the most painful and most expensive part of the transition. It's also the most necessary in order to pass, even more than your voice and the size of your hands. A male-to-female transsexual can walk into a store with her hands cupped and not say a word, but she can't hide her five o'clock shadow."

Laser can work in the early stages, but not over time.

When she tells me what Patty does—something with a needle and a pedal and red-hot electricity into a pore—I can hardly bear to hear the details. It takes eight hours a day, four days in a row. Some parts of the body—not the ones you'd necessarily think were extra-sensitive—are more painful than others. Invading the skin under the nose and around the lips is so excruciating that when she comes to another body part, the lesser pain seems almost soothing.

But Ellen tells me with delight that Patty says she's the most normal one of everyone she's treated.

" 'You were born to be a chick,' she told me."

For comportment she has found Denae, a widely recognized expert, an ex-model who teaches her clients how to walk, sit, go through doorways. She works on "GGs" (Genetic Girls) as well as "Ts" (we're not allowed to say "natural" girls, just as adoptees are no longer distinguished from "natural" offspring). And she works on men as well as women, hetero and homosexual.

"There are," Ellen tells me, "say, twenty 'cues' for femininity: the face is first and foremost, by far the most important; then height, shoulders, hands, dress, voice, way of entering a room, and so forth. You can get nineteen right, but if one is off, it can ruin the whole effect. If the polish is too bright, the makeup attention-getting, not to mention the inescapable factors of height and voice, then you're *read*.

"The one thing they tell you is not to overdo it, yet it's the one thing most transsexuals do. It's hard because of the way women dress nowadays. In the seventies, it was men, with their bell-bottoms, sideburns, Afros, who looked a little ridiculous, while women looked good. Now it's the opposite, the only women who wear skirts to the grocery store are the ones who've come from a PTA meeting or the boardroom. I can't do grunge," says Ellen. "I couldn't as a man, and can't as a woman.

"This terror of going among strangers—a woman, I think, would have a harder time understanding this, or feeling this, than a man. They might understand it on a mental level. They can put on men's clothes. They can go back and forth even. But for a man, the ones I have talked to told me they could never do it. They would absolutely jump off a bridge before they'd do that type of thing. About the only thing worse I can imagine would be to be buried alive. Every once in a while you read about someone who is kidnapped and put in a coffin in the ground with a breathing tube. Next to that . . ."

But what an image!

Yet, some of the fear comes from the sight, and ridicule, of those transsexuals who haven't had the advantage—because either they were born too soon or haven't pursued instruction with the zeal of Ellen— of absorbing the twenty cues of dress and behavior. Too often, the desire to be "too" feminine outstrips taste and sense. I think of the sad but also hopelessly funny anecdote in Esther Williams's memoir of her brief love affair with Jeff Chandler. He was a very lusty and compatible lover whom she was about to marry when she went up to the bedroom one night and found him dressed in women's clothes. After finding a closet full of high-end frocks from Rodeo Drive, she threw him out, hurling the words: "You're much too big to wear polka dots."

Ah, dress. We can't get away from it.

"Same person. No difference at all. Just a different sex," observes Tilda Swinton's Lady Orlando in the movie.

And Virginia Woolf in the book: "Different though the sexes are, they intermix. In every human being a vacillation from one sex to the other takes place, and often it is only the clothes that keep the male or female likeness, while underneath the sex is the very opposite of what it is above."

Woolf would probably agree with Alison Lurie, who pointed out in *The Language of Clothes* that we provide a reading of ourselves through the way we dress that is likely to be truer and more revealing than our speech. And the messages are often contradictory, not because they "intermix" male and female, but because of another fundamental struggle, that between modesty and the desire for attention.

Orlando's voyage is, among other things, a disguised valentine to lesbianism, or perhaps more delicately, to Sapphic love and androgynous freedom. Her ambisexuality also expresses the hunger of a strenuous ("masculine") mind in a female body to find a place in the world, but as a female who wouldn't have to suffer the insults and condescensions of men. But perhaps above all, Orlando's fluidity as a character is based at least as importantly on her ability to move through history, and to change location and occupation as easily as sex. Her endless mutability speaks to a fantasy of living without limits, even without death. Does the transsexual secretly annoy us by her hubris? By daring to be *both*?

Ellen has in common with other transsexuals of her type that she is not out to challenge the boundaries, the "categories." The basic assumption by "postcolonial" intellectuals is that having made a fetish of sexual difference, we require these figures of dubiety to perform a service by confusing and blurring gender. In this value system, the transgressive is both aesthetically and morally superior to that which is (or claims to be) stable, which is always seen as illusory or false.

Jan Morris is praised for provocatively asserting, "What if I remain an equivocal figure?" But Morris didn't exactly remain equivocal.

What Morris is not is "earnest," the unpardonable sin. Generally the transsexual is all too sincere; there is too much fear and anxiety to make room for irony.

Perhaps it is this desperation that unsettles. Zadie Smith, in an unusually harsh critique of *Transamerica*, takes the academically fashionable view. Why, she asks, if transsexuality is (as one character in the film attests) a " 'radically evolved state of being,' " does Bree want to take her doubleness and "reduce it to a singularity?" Wittily and almost incidentally, she goes on to what may be the real heart of the matter: dress. She laments Bree's "icky wardrobe of light pink separates and chiffon neckerchiefs, a Harry Belafonte basso and the prickly vulnerability of the permanently self-conscious." And in a last stand for multiculture and multiple identity, she righteously observes that Bree's journey "was never intended to genuinely challenge ideas of female beauty or femininity itself or gender dysmorphia or the surgery." And just what form would that challenge take? A protest at *Vogue* magazine, a mass burning of cosmetics? After all, in the real world we have to plunk down as one or the other, register as M or F in school, and on all legal documents thereafter. Moreover, it would seem the transsexual really does raise a great many questions, not so much about gender as about taste and snobbery and class that take cover behind these ideological catchwords.

Ellen will come to visit us next March, but now it's August, and on the fifteenth the envelope with photos arrives. I'm in the Long Island town of Quogue, at Round Dunes, a co-op where we have a little studio apartment on the beach. Mother had bought it in the midseventies and eventually given it to Andrew and me. It was my summer sanctuary. I'd live and work here and Andrew would come out weekends. It was midweek and, alas, I had no Andrew here to screen the pictures. I've been told by Eleanor that the visit with Barbara went well, and she thinks Ellen looks like me! After postponing the unveiling by performing one distracting chore after another, I finally open the envelope. First, I feel huge relief. Then pleasure. (See photograph on cover.) She looks so good, and it's not just the face and hair (okay, a little too blond) but the expression, the smile (not at all self-conscious), and the sheer delight it conveys. And that sweetness, always in him, seems to come quite naturally to the surface, to inhabit her face. A kind of unfurling. She looks—*together*, at harmony with herself. Nevertheless, as happy (and therefore reassuring) as she looks, I'm still nervous at the prospect of her coming up in March for the first time. Will I tell the doorman? No. I'll have to tell Esmey, our housekeeper who's been with us ever since we moved into our apartment in 1975. Originally from Trinidad, she's married (without children) and living in Brooklyn. She and Andrew and I are very close, have gone through one another's illnesses and losses. Friday always begins with the kind of ritual Andrew so loves. Esmey arrives, annoyed at her husband, Andrew greets her with some funny story or remark, and she laughs so hard that she's soon bent over, and then without even knowing what Andrew said, I begin laughing, too. She knows my brother and his wife, knew my mother, and will be knocked back on her heels. She's a smart, open woman, but—I sense—fairly conservative on "alternate lifestyle" issues.

Then Ellen moves the date up, says she's now planning to come in early January. Andrew asks, "Do I hug her?" Did you before? "No." Then no, I guess.

CHAPTER TEN

Ellen Becomes a Mountain Woman

I am woman, hear me roar.

—Helen Reddy

*T*here's nothing like a transsexual to bring out one's latent fashion snobbery, not to mention the equally ignoble if all-too-human worry "What will people think!" We may get past the either/ors of gender, even the blacks and whites of race, but never the ins and outs of fashion. The next couple of years will be a period of testing for Ellen and for me, and I think it's safe to say that she will pass more easily than I.

Ellen is supposed to come up in January, but her visit is delayed: I have emergency surgery for a bowel obstruction. These episodes—pain, hospitalization, abdominal surgery—have been the plague of my adult life. Ellen calls. She's concerned. Had the prospect of her arrival had anything to do with it? No, no, I reassure her. So it's to be February.

D-Day. Ellen comes! It is February of 2007, her first time in New York in the year and a half since the Announcement visit. Ever considerate, and not wanting to put undue stress on us, she's flown all the way up just for the day. The doorbell rings; Dmitrij, the steadfast doorman, announces my "sister." (I don't detect confusion or mirth in his voice.) And lo and behold, there she is, standing in the doorway with a big grin on her face. I still see my brother behind this . . . this . . . woman's face. We hug. She and Andrew shake hands. She looks radiant. She looks very blond. I scrutinize her colors, hair, dress, yet how reliable is my vision? It's like a cubist painting or Duchamp's *Nude Descending a Staircase*, a person in successive sections. I'm trying to see her as others will, but my view is inevitably colored by my own rainbow of emotions: hope, ambivalence, love, anxiety. The ambivalence revolves around her being both familiar and unfamiliar: though I wish ardently for her success as a woman, for my sake as well as hers, the more of a woman she is—or so it feels—the less of my brother there will be.

She has on some kind of white down jacket, bright blue turtleneck, and embroidered coat; her makeup is very subtle except for the bright pink lipstick. Very un–New York. But not Southern as I know it, either. (This shade, she'll tell me later, was chosen with a consultant.) Teeth very white, wig very blond, and quite a bit of hair. She is pretty, I think, not sure. Most of all she looks happy. My gaze stops before I get to the hands and feet; can't cope with it all yet. So I have no idea at all if she "passes," and if so, to what extent. All I can see is my brother not quite behind but coexisting with the mask. As it happens, Megan, our wonderful physical therapist, is here for her appointment with my husband, an inveterate couch potato before they invented the term. Even before the debilities caused by the illness of 1984, he spent more time prone than upright, a thinker and talker who lived in his head.

Megan, this dark-haired Irish beauty, provokes, prods, and charms Andrew into what are for him remarkable feats of effort and exertion.

Megan and Ellen shake hands and chat. I watch nervously. She gives her a thumbs-up. When she comes the following week, before I can ask her for her impression, she volunteers: "I didn't see a man when I saw her. She's very pretty, high cheekbones like you. And those blue eyes." But what about the hair? I ask. Megan pauses and admits she thought it wasn't a great wig, like someone receiving chemotherapy, "and you can get such good wigs now." Ellen, when I ask, tells me she's not happy with it, but it cost a thousand dollars! She wonders if they don't rip off transsexuals.

Next time Ellen comes I'll introduce her to the Witches. We're four close friends who walk around the reservoir every Tuesday and Thursday mornings, then go to Le Pain Quotidien for cappuccino. Lily, Fran, Patty, and I—dubbed by Patty "the Witches"—have developed a unique bond, like friendships at college with their continuous and uninterrupted rhythm. Unlike most New York relationships, nothing has to be compressed into an appointment, squeezed in over lunch or on the phone; everything gets aired and discussed: books, movies, politics, gossip, and whatever's ailing our bodies and minds at the moment. Patty is writing a book about the influence of Schiaparelli in her life; Fran's an ingenious and creative dresser; and Lily, who grew up in France and Italy, is the epitome of European chic. How will Ellen strike their style-savvy eyes?

In late February, accompanied by Eleanor, she will have the genital surgery, moved up to accommodate the doctor's schedule and also because she is deemed highly qualified by the two therapists required to evaluate her mental state, her preparedness. It normally takes a year, but she's such a good candidate, the two therapists give her a thumbs-up in terms of how realistic her expectations are, her mental health.

The surgery, with Eleanor accompanying her to Arizona, involves a vaginoplasty and (four months later) a labioplasty. Reader, be warned. Since I've already provided graphic details of the facial reconstruction, it seems only right to describe the genital one as well. But as they say on the news before showing pictures of carnage in the Middle East: some of these images may be shocking. As Ellen explains it—and here I force myself to switch to detached, biology-class mode—they first separate the head of the penis from the shaft but keep it attached for the nerves and blood vessels. Then they take the shaft and split it, removing the insides (discarded, or perhaps, as Ellen conjectures, shipped to the Far East as a delicacy), and make a cavity in the pelvic area for the vagina. They then turn the skin of the penis inside out, to form the wall of the vagina. For the labia, they use the penis head to form the clitoris. The scrotum is then removed, followed by the testicles, and the skin of the scrotum becomes the labia. There's some fine-tuning, plus another follow-up visit (Ellen will go alone), just as with the facial reconstruction. "It's as if you begin and end life as female," Ellen says.

Despite our inclination to recoil from such details, the procedure is actually far simpler and less painful than the facial reconstruction, and proceeds uneventfully and with satisfaction to all except Eleanor. For her it was heartbreaking, "the real last step," she tells me. "Until then, believe it or not, I still felt he might change his mind, go back to being John."

For Ellen it was a triumph: the test among transsexuals is that if done right, neither your lover nor your gynecologist will know. (This presuming it's a superficial exam.) She visits her gynecologist—and passes the test.

By now she's accustomed to "presenting" as a woman and so ready to reach out to fellow residents of Pine Mountain. Having come upon a notice on the bulletin board of a women's group that meets monthly for talk, book discussion, sometimes a speaker, she calls the head of it, tells her she's a transsexual and would like to participate, but doesn't want to offend anyone or make life awkward. Could the woman think about it and talk to the others? She does, they all vote to include her, and she's become a regular member of Mountain Women. She also volunteers at the Nature Foundation, providing information, leading hikes.

I'm invited to give a talk at a women-in-film weekend at Kripalu, the yoga center in Stockbridge, Massachusetts. Being a sometime yoga practitioner if not devotee, I leap at the chance. The accommodations are even more minimal than I'd expected. At the reception desk, arriving guests are greeted with neither key nor candy but a bowl of ear plugs. People pay princely sums for dorm rooms with no locks on the door, no phone, a "reading" lamp with barely the wattage of a nightlight. Inmates pepper the beautiful meadows like roaming cows, in search of cellular signals to the outside world. Activities other than yoga are discouraged, as are material possessions except those purchased at the abundantly stocked gift shop.

At the panels and talks, personal experiences are more in demand than critical analysis; the communal gatherings are predictably new-agey, and full of deep breathing and Women-on-Women bonding, celebrating our wonderfulness. Other than meeting the fabulous Jane Alexander, the most interesting moment for me comes at the end of our last session, a panel on women who make movies. The talk from the podium has concluded, the discussion is petering out, when a large elderly woman in a pants suit comes to the front of the room.

"I can't believe I'm doing this," she says, haltingly. "My name is Jenny Stevens. This week I heard the spirit of enlightenment, the excitement of possibilities for women expressed in totally positive terms . . . by everyone but me. We talked about hope for the future of women, and I probably appreciated that more than any of you, because I have chosen to spend more of my life as the woman I have always been. This is the first time I've said it in front of any group: I am a transsexual woman." She went on to describe the choices she'd made and the pain to herself and others (as a businessman with a family). She'd felt early on that the traits of the feminine gender, both good and bad (more caring, loving, intuitive, if also more bitchy), were those she wanted and needed.

"I want to move into the ranks of the active now," she said, and concluded, "My favorite song used to be 'I Enjoy Being a Girl!' and now it's 'I Am Woman (Hear Me Roar).'"

At first silence, then an eruption of applause and cheers, bringing tears to her eyes. Members of the audience rush to embrace her, and amidst the general celebration and "right-ons!" there are murmurs of "I thought so," or "I sat by her at lunch and I was wondering." She's seventy, closer to the ex-linebacker T than the "stealth" T—i.e., one young and/or pretty enough to "pass." Her voice is simply a raspy older person's voice, which in a way is more neutral than Ellen's. She's so engaging, so happy to be among sympathetic sisters, that the delight speaks for itself. She appears neither surprised nor annoyed when some of the attendees tell her they'd suspected she was a transsexual. The one word everyone uses (as they do when hearing of my brother) is "bravery." Yes, it takes courage to go through with it, to risk exposure, ridicule, and danger. But to Ellen, like Jenny, it doesn't feel as much like bravery as realism—a last chance to get things right, bring the inner and outer self into alignment.

After the hullabaloo has died down and people start to drift out, I approach her and confide my own tale. She greets me as a comrade-in-arms. We become fast friends as she describes some of her own experiences and asks about my sibling's.

She explains now, and in subsequent e-mails, that she and—probably—Ellen are "secondary" transsexuals in that "the urge keeps growing as we get older and begin to understand ourselves and our journeys. The primary transsexual is one who recognizes it very early and can make the transition easier in every way, especially physically."

In earlier years she had considered genital surgery because she wanted a man, "although as a man I wasn't necessarily gay . . . perhaps bisexual. But I wanted a man as any woman wants a man . . . to totally surrender (at least sexually). But by the time I recognized that fact, I had family, business, and other considerations that made it impossible."

Some things annoy, some break my heart. Sometimes they're the same thing. It's the spring of 2007. Eleanor's son has a jazz gig—he's a guitarist. Ellen would like to come. Adam's a fairly open guy but his boss and his wife will be there, and Eleanor says he's just not ready to make introductions. I'm ashamed for all of us, but . . . it's just too soon!

Later that spring, the same tricky situation presents itself to me. I have a lecture engagement at the University of Richmond in April, and Ellen wants to attend. She says she would just stand at the back of the room. But I'll be staying with Eleanor, and while neither of us is comfortable with the idea of Ellen coming to the lecture, for Eleanor it's worse. Her house is two blocks from the university and many of her friends and mine will be in attendance. This will be only the second time I've seen Ellen, and we haven't yet appeared in public together. I remind her that Beth's tolerance and openness are not the standard reaction.

"Reactions have been all across the spectrum," she insists. "The people at Pine Mountain, the working people, are fine with it. Some of these—the woman who does my manicure-pedicure, the cleaning woman, and others—have become friends."

To me that's a slightly different matter. The ever-thoughtful Ellen says, "Do what causes the least stress," which of course makes me feel a surge of guilt for excluding her. She wants so much to be accepted, but she can't just "slip in." And so we agree she won't come to this one but will to the next.

Eleanor says people are "reading" Ellen and she doesn't realize it. Possibly, but isn't this another necessary form of denial? We all wear blinders of one kind or another, else how would we get through each day? And for the transsexual, all it takes is one remark out of the mouths of babes, and—poor naked emperor—the sham is exposed. It's no wonder children pose a constant threat. Not yet initiated into the adult conspiracy of silence, the oracular child gives voice to what his or her elders are thinking, or almost thinking. Renée Richards (in *No Way Renée*) writes of what I now think of as a *Transamerica* moment. She is somewhere, having a "bad voice" day, and a child asks her mother, "Why is that man wearing a dress?" Over the many insults she's endured, she continues to remember this one disproportionately, and realizes, "I must have missed a great many subtler cues, thanks to my capacity for self-deception"—a self-deception that she sees, and I see, as a form of self-preservation. If she, or Ellen, were to notice and feel every curious eye, every disdainful glance, how could either go forward? Ellen tells me that she *was* anxious in the beginning but then decided to believe that everyone "read" her, which was enormously freeing. She acknowledges that those who knew her before will always see Chevey inside Ellen, but strangers have told her that if they hadn't heard her voice they would never have known.

I dream constantly, and most involve someone who looks like Chevey metamorphosing into a woman, sometimes Ellen, sometimes another woman, then back again, while great anxiety revolves around a trip to Richmond that the three of us—or perhaps I should say four of us—are to take. But then role reversal was a recurring theme in my psychoanalysis: my analyst, male, often became a woman in my dreams. Was this some version of my strong mother, or was my unconscious preparing for this day?

I go down to Richmond to give my lecture and take a taxi to Eleanor's, where I will be staying. Ellen has come down for the day so the three of us can have lunch together and she greets me at the door. I do a double take. As deeply in tune as we are, the sight of her never ceases to startle. Yet I'm happy the three of us are together and it seems to go pretty well. But when I return to New York, Eleanor calls and says she just can't see Ellen anymore. It's too wrenching.

"Every time I see her I see my husband, and it's killing me. I told her I want to go on having a relationship with her but only on the phone or e-mail."

And that's how they communicate for the next two and a half years. Ellen will come down from time to time to pick up papers she's stored in the office. She'll arrive at a scheduled time, locate her files and documents, read Eleanor's list of computer and household problems, and check them off. Then, at the appointed time, Ellen will depart, and Eleanor will return fifteen minutes later.

When they finally start seeing each other again, it will be at the urging of Barbara and Adam, who make Eleanor understand there will be important moments in their lives and they'll want Ellen to be there. And Eleanor realizes that it would be better to have some sort of reconciliation before those events, so she won't be caught off guard.

I understand. Even as I become accustomed to Ellen, in conversation, I'll reflexively say "he," and when she resumes her old voice on the telephone, I happily picture her as male. I can't let go of my brother, and apparently I'm not alone. Esmey has never been able to call her "she." Ellen's friends from the old days, she tells me, all prefer to hear the Chevey voice (or that voice in an only slightly higher register). There seem to be several registers now, the baseline (which she uses with me) is slightly higher than her old voice, while the new one, higher and of a different timbre, she must work to maintain. It's fatiguing, like speaking a foreign language, and she lapses. Beth's sister says that Ellen's so totally changed outwardly, the "Chevey" voice is the one link to the man she knew.

. . . .

My summer and fall of 2007 are consumed by work, and there's very little about Ellen in my journal. I complete a manuscript, turn it in, and prepare to endure the yearlong, multiphased agony that is book-birth, one to which other anxieties are temporarily subsumed.

For Ellen, the spring and summer of 2008, after the terrible and trying previous year, are a resounding success.

Back at Pine Mountain after the follow-up genital surgery, she's become part of a hiking group and tells me that she recently went swimming with some twenty people, men and women, in a cold lake. Whoa there! Swimming? In a bathing suit? Yes, she answers. For some reason, this stops me cold, more than any of the surgeries, which remain slightly abstract as all surgeries do. My brother, now dickless, in a woman's bathing suit.

And then another startling revelation: she now wants me to write the book. To help others in her condition, she says, and their families.

Another rather astounding piece of news is her happiness at Pine Mountain, where she has formed friendships with many of the "Mountain Women," and there are invitations back and forth for parties and outings. She's "making her place," as Mother would say. Because her apartment has a perfect view of the fireworks, she's having people over for the Fourth of July. Everyone will bring food; she doesn't want it too "planned." She even takes up tennis. I tell friends that although Mother would have had a heart attack at the news of Chevey's trans-sexualism, Ellen has become the kind of person Mother always wanted Chevey to be: social, a tennis player. She's "come out" in all senses of the expression: become more gregarious. It always struck me that Chevey and Eleanor had very little social life. Did this stem from his own sense of inauthenticity and the effort of "playacting" the conventional male? I wondered.

It wasn't that he was antisocial or even shy. He was good with people, friendly, at ease, a good teacher—the various caretakers who helped Mother in her last years all adored him. But there was something withheld, not exactly a barrier, but a polite reserve that discouraged intimacy.

Andrew liked Chevey immensely but always thought him guarded. He interpreted it as the protective strategy my brother had adopted after our father's death; a defense against being caught off guard by tragedy again. I'd thought so, too. As we grew up, putting years between ourselves and the trauma, I always felt a sadness or sorrow, a special vulnerability, where Chevey was concerned. Perhaps it was my own unexpressed grief projected onto him, but it came with guilt attached.

A memory: I am taking the train back to New York after a visit to Richmond, possibly following the Christmas of 1962 or '63, having only recently become a New Yorker. Chevey and Mother have driven me to Broad Street Station, the glorious vaulting neoclassical structure of so many childhood memories (now converted into a science museum), one of the Union Stations that connected the modern, industrial United States at the turn of the last century. In that cavernous echoing space, with its marble floors and walls, giant wood benches, we came and went, departed as a family on trips to Florida or North Carolina, or I alone to camp. Its grandeur lay not only in its architecture but in the links it forged with other parts of the country and those other Union Stations, some given local names, in Philadelphia, Chicago, Washington, D.C., Los Angeles, New York (Penn Station), Toronto, beckoning, haunting like the whistle of a train in the night, the conductor's cry.

But the excitement is always threaded through with an aura of sadness and melancholy, the little deaths of good-byes. This one I remember especially for the heavyheartedness I felt (and still feel, thinking of it) as I pulled out of the station, waving, watching Mother and Chevey dwindle in size, an aching reminder of our forlornness without husband and father.

Before his death we were four, we were strong. Now we are a vulnerable three, not just one number less, but exponentially diminished. We haven't found a way to arrange ourselves around the void. And with my leaving, there are only two, standing on the platform, growing smaller and smaller and sadder and sadder as the steam curls upward and the wheels gather speed. And I am feeling guiltier and guiltier for abandoning them. Possibly I can't bear my own sense of aloneness, of not belonging to one place or the other. But somehow all of this sadness concentrates on Chevey, who is seventeen but seems like a lost little boy who can't be reached. I realize I have always felt he was fragile in some unaccountable way.

Into this memory feeds an earlier incident from several years before, when I arrive from college for the Christmas holiday. We've come down in the world, having sold our handsome French Provincial house on Paxton Road and rented a tiny frame box from St. Stephen's Church. The holiday—the three of us, without Daddy, and in "straitened circumstances"—promises to be sad enough, but while Mother and I are decorating the Christmas tree, Chevey announces that he's volunteered for holiday duty at the filling station where he is working temporarily. So what little cheer we might have mustered is dispelled: Christmas becomes a day not of togetherness but of rejection. As Chevey made clear in that conversation with Mother and me, we didn't *know* him—didn't know who he was outside the family, didn't know he had a sense of humor. This sense of alienation, even the shortage of humor, might track back to those long years of Daddy dying, when we were locked in our private hells, unable to comfort one another, or not knowing how. It stemmed no doubt from some crazy WASP mixture of stiff-upper-lip stoicism and not wanting to burden each other. But that sense of love mixed with helplessness, of mutual abandonment, seems to circulate among us like a fog in which we're unable to see and feel one another clearly. It's no wonder we are relieved—and guilty—to get away.

We talk about not only the surgery but the other factors in her transition, the electrolysis (painful, continuing) and her comportment guide, both on the West Coast. In the summer of 2008, I'm very anxious about Andrew. He's so wobbly on his feet, he will need a walker soon, and, as I write in my journal, "He's so diminished in different ways, conversationally withdrawn, not 'getting' who people are, even actors in movies and on television." Is this just old age? He had the most phenomenal memory and even with this deficit retains more than most people. Yet the lapses are strange. And he doesn't seem perturbed the way most of us are. By anything. My journal is filled with cries of exasperation and anger. Some of this could be from terrible hearing and deteriorating vision, but his memory, his responsiveness to cinema, is who he is. Was?

In the fall of 2008 I'm planning his eightieth birthday party, on October 31. I don't invite Ellen, as I'm not quite up to the task of introducing her to so many friends at once. But in November the time seems right, and she comes for a visit and finally gets to meet some friends.

Ellen will arrive on a Wednesday and stay three nights. Before she comes I mention (as tactfully as I can) the jeans with the appliqué flowers and wonder if she has another pair. She says yes, she already knew my feelings about them (oops!), but "a lot of people love them."

First, it's Betty and Jeanne, the two she already knows, who come for lunch (during which time Andrew is walking the halls and lifting barbells with Megan). Jeanne looks agreeably surprised, smiles with pleasure at seeing her. Betty, the onetime actress (and television reporter), stops dead in her tracks. "I'm speechless," she says, which she actually is for about forty-five seconds. "I expected a nice, middle-aged woman. Instead I got a looker!" Where once she might have begged off, Ellen now likes meeting people, both known and unknown, and seems to regard these encounters as a kind of test she almost relishes. She wants to know people's reactions (the *truth*, she says), and whether she's "read" or not, she likes and is proud of her new body, her new self.

She's more than willing to reveal the gaffes and absurdities. She tells Betty and Jeanne the story of going to a boutique to try on clothes. She's decked out in a very nice jacket, and thinks she looks pretty good, but then something gets twisted or caught. "Shit," she explodes in a clearly male voice.

But when we're alone, she tells me, "I think a lot about how incredible it is being Ellen, especially in those early months. It's probably the most terrifying thing I could imagine happening, short of certain life-threatening situations. It was exhilarating and terrifying at the same time. Even when you have been in therapy and the people closest to you know about it, when the time comes and you actually have to put on women's clothing and go out in public . . . you've practiced, you've been coached, you've done all kinds of things, you've had two or three people teach you about clothes and makeup, but then you go out and do it."

I'm reminded of the "twenty cues for femininity" and the terror of being "read."

Next morning, the Witches. I'm worried it might seem as if I were introducing her like the freak come to town. She says no, they're your good friends and if I were your brother you'd want me to meet them. This is true. I've gradually met most of Lily's vast brood of children and stepchildren, grandchildren and in-laws and an ex-husband, though I've never met Patty's sister who lives in Florida (I will, eventually) or Frannie's brothers. Fran is away, so it's only Patty and Lily. Ellen's a fervent walker but hasn't brought sneakers so doesn't accompany us around the reservoir. We pick her up, she looks fine in plain pants and a white parka with faux-fur trim, and at Le Pain Quotidien everyone seems to get along well. She is utterly at ease, and more to the point, she puts them at ease. I ask her to tell us about the ways men and women do things differently, and she demonstrates: women hold their hands open, a sign of submission, while men's closed hands signify aggression. (Like two dogs squaring off, the smaller bowing to the larger.) Women are more closed, there's no space between the arms and the body when they walk, whereas a man walks more openly, moving his shoulders. She swaggers in exaggerated Neanderthal style to demonstrate. She has learned how to minimize her shoulders with jewelry or collars. She tells them the nightmare fantasy she told me about, that she will be strolling in the Village shopping center and a young mother with her child will come by and the child will say, "Mommy, why is that man dressed as a woman?"

Later Patty asks me why I made her talk about it, as if I'd pumped her for their benefit. Was I tactless, putting her on display out of my own nervousness? But she's always happy to talk about it, and the subject's so fascinating. It seems to me I elicit all this because I know they're interested, and I know she's willing to discuss it. Also, this openness and personal candor is such a welcome difference from the more guarded pre-Ellen Chevey. Is this because endocrines have made her more "female," or because she's simply happier and more at ease? Having "come out" and made the change, the person that is ChivEllen (as I call her to myself, and shorthand as C/E in my writing) *can* be open now? This is what I've learned: how well she handles it all. From what she's told me about a few trips she's taken with small groups, if someone seems curious, gives any kind of cue, she'll open up. Otherwise, she won't bring it up.

The verdict from the Witches after Ellen's departure: she's very convincing. I said the hair's too blond, and Lily and Patty agree, the hair is too blond, but they're surprised at how good she looks and most of all how happy she seems.

What Ellen treasures from the occasion is something else. At coffee, Patty referred to the moment when the three of us came to the lobby to get her. "We walked through the front door," Patty said, "and I looked all around and couldn't find you; I just saw this woman there."

Ellen tells this with enormous pleasure, but then, "What do you think she expected?" she asks ruefully.

CHAPTER ELEVEN

Ellen Changes Her Mind, and Changes It Again

He wanted to be like his mother and now he is his mother.
—Dr. Fred Richman (of Norman Bates) in *Psycho*

I feel like someone who died and came back to life in a different form.

—Ellen

She's cute; she looks just like your mother.

—Esmey

I go down to visit Ellen after Christmas in 2008, almost two years after I first saw Chevey as Ellen. She's wearing her Santa hat, enjoying her work at the Nature Foundation, and looks the picture of health. We compare notes. I'm on Imitrex (for migraines, a constant now) and various medications, including the occasional sleeping pill, while she takes no medications (only the estrogen patch), not even vitamins or aspirin. When she applied for health insurance as a transsexual, she was dropped from Category One down to Category Four (the most expensive), presumably because of her "condition." She wrote a letter pointing out that she was a far better risk than either a man or a woman, having no uterus, no ovary, no cervix, no penis, and a shrunken prostate gland. Even her old problem, high cholesterol, seems to have vanished with her superhealthy diet. A few months later she received her new insurance card. No letter, just the card. She'd been bumped back up to Category One.

Pine Mountain, where she lives, is a skiing and hiking community in the Appalachian Mountains. The complex consists of condos, town houses, single-family homes, some tucked in the woods, others, like Ellen's, angled into the mountain like birds' nests. Her two-bedroom apartment is on one of the highest peaks and has what she considers the best view: forty or fifty miles of mountains and valleys. The living room is an open space that includes the dining area and kitchen, and with its plaid-covered furniture surrounding a fireplace, has a comfortable ski-lodge look. A wall of sliding-glass windows leads to a balcony that looks out on two slightly smaller mountains and a valley 2,500 feet below. The ski lift (used all too infrequently in these snowless winters) threads its way down the hill.

Outside, natural beauty with discreet man-made intrusions. Inside, art and artifice, like the bar shelves displaying her collection of hand-carved wood birds and a sailing ship in artisan glass. On the mantel are artificial ivy, African violets, handcrafted plants, wildflowers that look about as real as artificial flowers get.

On this trip, I ask again about change and record the answers—it's now more than two years since the facial surgery, but of course she has been taking hormones since 2005.

"The treatment is much more sophisticated than it was when I first thought I was going to try and transition in 1978. Then, there was no estrogen as such, or rather estrogen in the form of the birth control pill, no testosterone blocker and nothing about progesterone. When I took birth control pills the first time around, I did experience a little swelling of the breasts. I had to get Ace bandages and wrap my chest. It wasn't a great solution, as the bandage would roll down during the day, and you have to adjust it."

"Was this when you were working at the brokerage house?"

"No, at this point I had moved into The Argonaut Company and it was summertime. Winter was not a problem, but in summer you wear a short-sleeved shirt, and if you have Ace bandages on, even skin colored, you can still see the outline. So I ended up wearing undershirts under short-sleeved shirts, I was so terrified of anybody seeing the Ace bandages, and even more of not wearing them. I probably walked stooped over.

"But that didn't last long. I realized the Ace bandage dilemma was just the tip of the iceberg, and even that I had to figure out on my own. At that point it would have been so awful for you and Mother and everyone else, it seemed my only choice was just to move away, disappear. Move to California because all the freaks went to California. And that's when I first started thinking I needed a different name, even a different last name. Some transsexuals change their first name and keep the family name. I was so afraid that even if I moved to California, people would find out.

"Now I have an estrogen patch and the amount of hormones can be adjusted regularly. It's hard to separate changes from hormones from the normal changes of aging; for instance, the hair on my body seems a little finer, but it's hard to measure. As I mentioned before when I talked to the endocrinologist, he said: you'll notice some mental changes, you'll feel differently about things. He made me think my thought processes would completely change, my body less so. But it happened in just the opposite way! His idea always sounded wrong to me; it didn't change my way of thinking. I don't think he understood it all very well. When I went to my therapist, I mentioned I was supposed to feel more feminine, but I didn't feel any different, and he said, 'You were that way before.' "

· · · · · · ·

When Andrew and I go to Miami in January 2009, he says this is probably our last trip here together. While there, he's almost too tired to go to the movies, sleeps all the time. It seems to me he's not all "there" anymore.

Back in the spring of 2008, Ellen decided she wanted me to write the book. I had been taking notes all along, and with a feeling of excitement and collaboration we began compiling transcripts of interviews. Now it's the summer of 2009, I am in Quogue, working on a draft, outlining a proposal, when, in a phone conversation, she says she's changed her mind. There are two things that bother her: the privacy issue and her reluctance to "negotiate" with me, her sister. What do you mean? I ask, but I know what she means. She doesn't want to be going over the manuscript, wanting this and that deleted, while I defend my position. I'm utterly crushed, desperate, but maybe some small part of me is relieved. Still, I stop in my tracks, fall into a depression.

Then, in November, we're planning a rendezvous. I have to give a lecture in Norfolk, so we'll meet in Williamsburg for the weekend, where we'll have rooms at her favorite hotel, the Williamsburg Lodge. Before I leave New York we have one more conversation: "I've thought about it some more," Ellen says. "I do want you to write the book. I want to help people. I wish there had been such a book for me."

I'm thrilled, beyond thrilled. "But," she adds, "I have a few stipulations." We agree to go over them in Williamsburg. (I knew I wouldn't get off scot-free. How much control will she want? How much can I afford to concede?)

I call when I get there. It's a full four years since the original announcement to Andrew and me, yet this is my first encounter with her in public. I'm acutely self-conscious—far more, it seems to me, than she! Every time we exit or enter the hotel, effusive doormen in colonial garb say, "Good morning, ladies," "How are you, ladies?" and I do a double take. Yet the theatricality provides protective cover: it somehow makes it easier that our first public get-together is in this eighteenth-century theme park where tourists mingle with actors and volunteers impersonating early Americans. I soon discover that old habits die hard. Every time we go through a door, I walk in front of her as I would if she were a man. Then my worst gaffe: we're at a high-end restaurant where "Rob," our waiter for the evening, has been hovering. I've just tasted Ellen's dish, then mine, and when Rob inquires I say enthusiastically, "His is good, but mine is great!"

Gulp. I'm mortified. Ellen gives a little laugh, then so do I. She's charmingly unvexed, yet I vow to be a little more on guard, hoping her her-ness will become second nature, a reflex. Do others "read" her? I don't want to know, not this trip. I think there are occasional glances, but do they just see two tall blondish women, possibly striking just for that, or because they resemble each other? Or something else?

The next day we're walking along the commons and during some intense discussion we stop and pause. I turn and look up at her, and I stop breathing. Mother! In that moment, Ellen *is* Mother. I don't see the hair or the makeup, the jewelry or the clothes. Just the face. It's as if I've dropped through the Looking Glass. Not *almost* Mother, and not just similar. But Mother. A chill runs through me; I almost call her "Mother." I'd thought there was a resemblance, but nothing like this. Maybe I'd been too aware of her size, the accoutrements, voice, clothes. Or had simply been too self-conscious to really look. But now, in this light . . . it's uncanny. And frightening. Freud gave us our modern idea of the uncanny as something already known that suddenly presents itself to us in unfamiliar form, akin to what the Russian formalist Viktor Shklovsky called a "defamiliarization." We shiver with a ghostly sense of recognition.

. . . .

I don't believe in the supernatural as embodied in current movies. Vampires, aliens, visitations by ghosts and extraterrestrials that shadow our worst (or best) selves, are patently phony, computer-generated images, props in an action story. But the world is full of spells and intuitions that move us like dreams, another level of reality. I think of the Celtic myth that the boy Marcel describes in *Swann's Way*—i.e., the belief that the souls of those whom we have lost are held captive in some animal or plant or inanimate subject, and are lost to us "until the day (which to many never comes) when we happen to pass by the tree or to obtain possession of the object which forms their prison. Then they start and tremble, they call us by our name, and as soon as we have recognized their voice the spell is broken. Delivered by us, they have overcome death and return to share our life."

My relationship with my mother was fraught and complicated—plenty of love but interludes of poisonous acrimony as well. Her death was both a sorrow and a relief, freeing me to remember her with a love drained of hate and anger. Now something very strange had happened. To put it bluntly, I'd finally gotten rid of my mother and now she had come back as my brother.

In looking back through some old journals, I find a dream recorded. This is 2002, and I have been toying with the idea of writing a memoir about Mother, more precisely about her dying. In the dream, I'm writing a novel. The "I" of the novel starts out as a woman, then turns into a man. While it's from his point of view, he remembers his son singing "Ave Maria" in a lovely soprano. He hums it, bringing it down a chord, end of novel.

Many cultures believe in the transmigration of the soul, also called *gilgul*, reincarnation. Ovid has Pythagoras say, "What we call death is when identity ceases." But it never does if one accepts the Hindu, Buddhist, or Kabbalist view of one's nonuniqueness in the chain of life.

I didn't think my brother and I were close, or that he was in my blood or my cells. I was so much older growing up, and we were so different: he loved nature and hiking, I loved books and cities and cafés; I was interested in art, he in everything else; when it came to food, I was both gourmand and gourmet (taking after our father), while sadly, Chevey didn't really enjoy, couldn't enjoy food (mostly because of a poor sense of taste, possibly attributable to the deviated septum, which the surgery had only partially ameliorated), and for him the greatest restaurant was a waste; he was both smart and informed about economics, while I couldn't fathom a Verizon bill and went into a nosedive of stress and dither over health-care choices, tax and insurance forms, and paperwork in general. He was patient, I was impatient.

But when I look back through family memorabilia, I find wonderful letters from him spanning different stages in our lives: loving, teasing, calling me nicknames, making jokes about his frugality. And I remember being with him on so many occasions—say, in a living room drinking coffee, when we would just sit in silence, in contemplative ease, with that special sense of being alone and not alone simultaneously. There was some kind of unspoken bond of blood or temperament; we knew without ever mentioning how alike we were in many ways, not least in sitting just so without the need for conversation. We were alike in our values, our responses, the things that irritated, amused, outraged, and delighted us, our reasoning in politics (mostly centrist, with he veering to the right and me to the left), things that made sense and didn't make sense.

I try to imagine a younger Ellen, twin sister to our mother, Mary the belle. Would she have been a heartbreaker? To those who met her, especially men, my mother had a siren-like allure. There was no single feature that leapt out at you. Blue eyes, but not startlingly so. Straight brown hair that drove her mad. In her flapper youth, curly hair was the rage. When the flu epidemic of 1918 caused the hair of some of the afflicted to spring into curls, my ten-year-old mother prayed to God to give her a case just serious enough to leave her with curly hair while sparing her life. It was one of the things she envied about me, though my frizzy, mousy hair could have been thought desirably "curly" only in her maternal eyes.

"I was never a beauty," she would say, and she almost had me convinced. Indeed, sometimes it was almost true. Unsmiling, or in repose, when her mouth turned downward, she could look ordinary, even old. But when she smiled, or became engaged, the eyes danced, she was bewitching.

"Mary has a fatal effect on men," wrote my aunt Sue when Mary Clark came up from North Carolina to a Richmond ball and added the heart of Sue's brother to those of half the bachelors in town. She loved to dance, would rather have danced than fall in love and marry. But her charm never managed to blunt her analytic mind.

When she married my father (also magnetic, and catnip for women), she embraced Richmond's politically conservative and socially gregarious life (and hoped her two children would, too). Yet her genetic heritage and parental influences were anything but conventional or straightforward, a DNA of warring impulses. Her father, a New Yorker, had antagonized his very formal banking family by enrolling in Columbia's engineering school. He'd invented a process for extracting turpentine from trees without killing them, had come South with the patent and fallen in love—with the South and with my grandmother.

Granny, tall, an expert horsewoman and bridge player, was more "handsome" than beautiful. She had gone to college and become a Latin scholar (very unusual for her time, the 1890s, and place: Fayetteville, North Carolina), then decided education wasn't for women and raised her daughter as a belle.

"I didn't want all those clothes," Mother would say, with a little rueful smile. This was the closest she would come to criticizing her mother.

Her life became a whirlwind of beaux. Balls, tea dances, nightclubs in New York, where she went to live and paint at the Art Students League. Dancing and painting, painting and dancing, these were her two passions. She didn't want to marry. She was terrified of sex, not to mention children and domesticity. But time was passing, the red shoes were wearing thin. Her adored older brother Frank warned her that she was at a dangerous age and shouldn't become a spinster. So instead of jumping off a cliff or in front of an onrushing train, she stopped like a sensible woman. There, standing in front of her when she came to rest, was my father. She married him.

There were doubts on both sides. My mother loved painting, loved her independence. A passionate letter from my father wonders in fact if she isn't too smart and independent for marriage. He writes that her allure is so powerful, men should be tied to the mast, like Odysseus, to avoid succumbing. When I read this, even more than the image, it was the literary reference that surprised.

Moreover, my mother's siren call to the opposite sex by no means involved excluding friendships with women. She was not one of those scheming beauties in Trollope of whom a rival might say, "She is one of those girls whom only gentlemen like." To which the wise old matron adds, "And whom they don't like very long."

Far from it. Not only was she a friend to other women, she was a missionary on their behalf.

It strikes me now that my fascination with roles came from her, from all the resistance she harbored. And from the strength that she and all those other "steel magnolias" couldn't quite conceal. I had assumed that the inspiration for my first book, a historical-polemical view of women's roles in the movies, came from feminism—the women's movement was such a huge catalyst and shaper of our lives in the early seventies. But I now see the converse was the case. It was my interest in roles that led me to feminism, which in turn led me to examine the subtext, the subconscious, to try to better understand the women of the thirties and forties, my mother's generation, so interesting and mysterious, so closed off from giving expression to their own ambivalences.

A lifelong cheerleader for women's independence, she pushed me toward self-reliance almost from the time I was born. When I was hardly more than a toddler, she'd send me into Lamston's ten-cent store and wait in the car for me to make a purchase. And before a school play, she'd have me stand across the room and shout my lines. From then on, I would always appear confident as a speaker, even if I was jelly inside.

When she spent summers in Quogue, she would urge the other ladies to come with her across the street to the rental tennis courts, and there she would teach them to play. Reversing the usual pattern, she had switched from golf to tennis in her mature years, and like Saul on the Road to Damascus, she not only had a "conversion experience," she became a proselytizer.

Around the same time as the tennis epiphany (she was about fifty), this ultrarational woman began to believe in reincarnation. Over the cocktail hour, which began early and ended—well, hardly ever—she'd speculate on what form her next life might take. Would she be a dog? An old man? And would we recognize each other? She imagined different future lives. In one eerily prophetic and politically astute hypothesis, she was going to wind up in the Middle East, with a specific place and mission in mind. "I'm going to Saudi Arabia," she said, "and teach the women to drive, and play tennis."

Though deeply distrustful of the supernatural, I could appreciate the generosity, even wisdom, of this impulse while smiling with the superior wisdom of the unbeliever, little suspecting that it would almost come true.

After I was born, she kept trying to have another child, preferably a boy. Or so she said and thought. But did she secretly want another girl she could bend and sculpt, coax like Silly Putty into something with form and substance? After all, she was an artist—a painter—who gave it up when she married my father. The paintings were hidden away; her talent was the madwoman in the attic. We children were her raw material. If a girl would provide more to work with, being both more amenable and more of a challenge, might there have been a struggle in the womb as the fetus, torn between male and female, emerged in a murky afterbirth of gender confusion?

In Williamsburg, we arrive at the negotiation stage. "It's *your* book," Ellen insists, and tells me I can say what I want to about her (yeah, right!), but she requests the veto power over anything that might hurt Beth or Eleanor. There's something about secondary rights. I sign it.

Later, we talk about why she changed her mind about wanting me to write the book. At the request of her therapist, she's met a number of would-be transsexuals, and they're all having a difficult time. Some simply don't know how to make a transition; or they face rejection, expulsion, estrangement from friends and family. She's clearly been moved by the depth of misery she finds. Many simply can't afford surgery, or even good makeup and clothes. Ellen has tried to do what she could, encourage them, provide emotional support, even assist them in buying the right cosmetics and women's wear. One man, though convinced he's a she, refuses to do anything to alter his rough male appearance. Then there's the man in his forties who wanted desperately to be accepted as a woman. Dealing with his urges was bad enough, but he was struggling alone, his large family—parents, siblings—having completely abandoned him. At one point, there seemed to be a thawing. His father called and invited him to a huge family reunion in the Bahamas, and our guy-gal was beside himself with joy. Acceptance at last, he thought, until his father called a week later and apologized, saying the trip had to be cancelled. A few months after that, he placed a call to his brother, only to be told by a secretary that her boss had gone on a family vacation in the Bahamas.

As heartbreaking as this story is, I'm grateful in that it has, I think, made the difference in Ellen's decision to have her story told. When Chevey told me in 2005 that as Ellen he'd still be the same person inside, and when Ellen told me the same thing, I accepted the truth of it, for certainly much is the same: the character, the humor, the empathy. But Ellen is not the same person. She's more open, more available, more trusting. The Chevey of 1994 and 2005 would never have let me write this book.

As it is, permission may be harder than prohibition. I shall feel her eyes on me, looking over my shoulder, and feel the burden of having to justify her trust as I collect, file away, take notes, hesitate, and procrastinate. The resistance comes partly from inhibitions about exposing my treasured sibling, even if she is now actively encouraging me, even participating in the project. Will I be able to write freely, even satirically, about my brother/sister, treat with some degree of humor a matter so touchy, so sensitive, so possibly injurious to the him that was becoming her? Not to mention the inevitable exposure of two very private people, my sisters-in-law. In sum, would love constrain me? Would conscientiousness weigh so heavily that it became a burden?

CHAPTER TWELVE

Andrew Falls and Ellen Comes Up and Shows Off Her Body

*I*n May of 2010 I go to Sweden, to the university at Norrköping, about two hours from Stockholm, where I've been invited to speak about film criticism and my book on *Gone with the Wind*. Norrköping is a charming surprise, a nineteenth-century manufacturing town that has been renovated and preserved, factories turned into museums, winding along a canal.

I fall in love with the place and my hosts, and it's a great relief to spend a whole week not having to talk about what I'm doing now, or my brother becoming my sister. I speak before an audience of faculty and students, and am surprised to find that more of them have read or seen *Gone with the Wind* than have read or seen *The Girl with the Dragon Tattoo*. Stieg Larsson seems to be more popular as an export, but I remark on the odd similarity between two "gender nonconformist" heroines. Scarlett O'Hara and Lisbeth Salander, though separated by a century and a half and radically different cultures, are sisters under the skin by virtue of their "masculine" qualities: narrowly focused brilliance, ruthless ambition, and a deafness to the usual social cues.

I've been home five days, and my world collapses once again. On a beautiful Saturday, Andrew and I are walking across Madison Avenue, on our way to the West Side to see a film and have brunch, when Andrew falls in the street and hits his head. He's fallen before but has usually made a soft landing, crumpling like a parachute. This time he crash-lands on his head. Bleeding in the street, bleeding in the brain.

The ambulance takes us to Lenox Hill Hospital, where, after the usual scans and MRIs, he's diagnosed as having a traumatic subarachnoid hemorrhage. This is the third brain injury, the first being the terrifying cytomegalovirus encephalitis in 1984, and the second a subdural hematoma after we were rear-ended in 2000. That one required surgery; this one fortunately doesn't.

While he's in Lenox Hill, Ellen arrives with her friend Sue for a long-planned, three-day theatre trip. They'll be staying at her recently acquired time-share in the Fifties near Seventh Avenue and close to the entrance of Central Park, a place Ellen loves to visit the way I love Paris. I've met none of her new friends and am immensely curious to meet Sue, her favorite. After a prearranged tour with a park expert and historian, they come for brunch, Ellen abuzz with descriptions of outlying areas of the park that I've never seen—and probably never will. Sue is remarkable, very attractive—sixtyish but looks fifty, was once a model but now has a comfortable middle-aged beauty. An avid reader and world traveller, she's divorced with grandchildren, now has a boyfriend, but refuses to remarry. Ellen's lucky to have her, but then she, I realize, is lucky to have Ellen.

Ellen's only here for a quick visit but takes time out to worry about Andrew, and about me and my health. In 1984, Chevey and Mother came alternately to stay at the apartment and help me during Andrew's illness, and I surely wouldn't have gotten through the ordeal without them. Ellen now advises me, as Mother used to, "Don't overdo it." (I always do, swinging from driven mode to collapse.) She tells me I need to save myself and should just go to the hospital once a day. Although this is clearly meant for my own good, it irritates me, just as it did in 1984. Why didn't he, why can't she, understand that I *have* to go twice a day?

In a Venus and Mars squaring-off, reason was Chevey's way as emotion was mine. It wasn't that he was unfeeling, but his rationality has always made him appear that way. I took it to be a carapace he'd developed when our father was dying, to defend against further trauma. But now I wonder: could it be the sort of coping mechanism therapists Mildred Brown and Chloe Ann Rounsley, authors of *True Selves: Understanding Transsexualism*, describe, whereby transsexuals relieve stress by visualizing, in their disturbing words, an "impenetrable shell or container, not unlike a steel vault, into which they deposit and lock away all of their cross-gender feelings, yearnings, dreams, behaviors and mannerisms." That's a lot to lock away, requiring a pretty thick wall. It might explain the isolation, the moat he dug around himself. The near-obsessive rationality.

After they were married, he and Beth moved to the country, to distance themselves from Richmond. Chevey seemed to be trying to carve out a space for himself with inviolable boundaries.

Once, after Andrew and I were married, the two came to New York but made a point of *not* making a date to see us. I kept waiting and waiting, and no word from Chevey. He'd spent a year in Manhattan after college, working for the New York branch of his firm, so he knew his way around. I could see how his mind worked. He wanted to establish a precedent; he could come to New York without necessarily "touching base" with us. Yet my understanding of his motives didn't make it hurt any less. When Andrew and I came back to the apartment (it was their last day in New York), there were Chevey and Beth sitting on a bench in the lobby, looking sheepish. It was a very cool, very brief encounter. "Dropping in" instead of making a date was part of his defense against being hamstrung by what he thought of as arbitrary, socially imposed duties to family. It wasn't an aversion to us per se (or so I prefer to think); moreover, other kinds of duties he willingly took upon himself. He simply detested what he saw as "social" obligations, the tyranny of blood ties, doing things for appearances, the imposed rules and expectations. He stirred up a furor in the family when he persuaded Mother to stop giving Christmas presents to all the cousins, who were by now in their thirties and had children of their own. We were too old for it, he insisted, and it was too much of a burden for her, now a widow with little time on her hands. The other family members were furious, but he was right, Mother was relieved, reason had triumphed.

As Mother aged, long before she was ill with emphysema, he took over all of her financial work, paid the bills, kept track, made who knows how many calls, did it all uncomplainingly. They had fun, too—he went out with her on her landscape-painting expeditions, carried her canvases and paints; helped her hang the pictures when she had shows; took slides of all of them. When she was dying—she lived now in the Tuckahoe Apartments, with round-the-clock aides—he behaved with his usual commonsense practicality, a tower of strength to the rest of us. It was this calm that led casual observers to think he might be indifferent. But I knew more was going on underneath, and I had a glimmer of it after Mother died, when he confessed that when he left after a visit, he would take the stairs instead of the elevator . . . and cry all the way down.

After eleven days in the hospital, Andrew is sent to rehab for what will lengthen into six weeks. I choose the nearest one that takes our health insurance, a place that turns out to be ghastly bordering on the Dickensian. It is, like so many others, a nursing home, gussied up with "rehab" to bring in additional revenue from those who won't go gently into the good night. Patients are assigned to floors that, like Dantean circles of hell, announce their status: the degree of difficulty (dementia or just disagreeable), the nature of their insurance (if any). Indignities and neglect vary according to floor, but ubiquitous are the terrible food, the overworked staff, the viruses and bacteria that leap from floor to floor and room to room, and the communal lunch hour when the patients, in a hapless display of wheelchair-bound togetherness, are assembled in the television room.

He finally comes home, now on a walker though delirious with joy, but he doesn't know where his pajamas are, doesn't remember to brush his teeth, or how to operate the remote or microwave, has to be told how to dial a number (put a one in front). Some of these are familiar symptoms of the Absentminded Professor syndrome, the techno-dummy, but intensified and magnified. Will some or all of this routine stuff come back? Can he go back to teaching at Columbia in a matter of weeks? Will I be able to live without him, or the him I knew? Will I be able to live with (and love) the new him?

In all of this, harrowing as it is, there's nothing special. Unlike the earlier out-of-the-blue crisis, this one is accompanied by the silent stalker: Old Age as the slow precursor to Death. What I'm going through is just what women married to older or infirm husbands do. That's what makes it so awful. It's what we *do*. I think we must come to despise our own strength, the role that's simply expected of us.

"You do what you have to do," or "You find out how strong you are," somebody will say, or think. But how often do we need to make that discovery?

By this time we're in late July and I want someone to take care of me. Friends are wonderful, but what can they do? It's a full-time job, and neither the emotional cross (the heaviness of heart, the constant dread and apprehension) nor the logistical minutiae are the sorts of burdens anyone else can assume.

I want my brother, the rock of reliability, the quietly take-charge person. But my brother is now my sister. Lucky for me, my newly minted sister is still the magnificent human being my brother was. But sexist as it sounds, I miss that male shoulder to lean on. Nine weeks into the ordeal I call her, and she instantly makes plans to come up. I cry with relief when I get off the phone, realizing only at that moment the extent of my longing for her calming presence. I still haven't gotten completely past the self-conscious stage, twinges of anxiety about how she will look and sound—to me, to others. But it's 2010 now, and it's gotten a lot easier in five years.

She comes up and stays at a nearby hotel. The first morning, I go to meet her at a café on Madison Avenue. I see her coming a block away and I cringe. She's wearing short shorts and a sleeveless top, her smooth legs and buff arms gleaming in the sun. She's definitely more Marilyn Monroe than Marilyn Manson, but is that a good thing? When I express horror, she contradicts me: they're not *short* shorts, they're exercise shorts, for walking in the park. I tell her she can wear them in the park but *not* on the street. Well, then, she wonders, how does she get from the hotel to the park?

This is the first chance I've had to look at this new body, and it has an eerie, ageless, almost sexless quality in its perfection. The skin is golden, smooth and consistent, no blotches, no blemishes, no spots. It might be a digitalized body in a movie, or a classical sculpture. She harks back to ancient Greek culture where the body was an idealized conception of beauty made visible. I imagine that if she had something covering her head and breasts, her hair and makeup, I wouldn't be able to tell if she was male or female. She would be just body, with a bird mask over the head like one of those Alexander McQueen mannequins in the Metropolitan that metamorphose into animals. In truth, she is on exhibit, the way she's outfitted herself, the casual exposure. Fortunately, her face, radiantly pretty, redeems the rest, or at least deflects from it.

. . . .

I have a gig at the Westhampton Fine Arts Theatre; they're showing *Agora*, with Rachel Weisz as Hypatia, the beautiful mathematician who lived in fourth-century Alexandria, and I'm to discuss it afterward with the series' regular host. Ellen and I take the Jitney out; this will be her first time at Round Dunes as Ellen. Chevey and Eleanor had visited in 2000, staying at a nearby bed-and-breakfast. It was the summer Andrew and I had had the automobile accident—how often Chevey's visits seemed to coincide with emergencies—and it was Eleanor who noticed the wayward gait that signaled the second massive brain injury.

They'd met a few friends at the time, including our neighbors the Deutsches, so I'm full of the usual mixed feelings: nervous about how Ellen will be perceived, exhausted from the aftermath of Andrew's disastrous fall, but relieved to be getting away and having time with, and help from, Ellen. She will wear a bathing suit, go to the beach, we'll have dinner with Nola and Stephen Deutsch.

And yet, I realize, I'm so much less nervous than I was a few years ago. The summer following the revelation, I lived in dread that the news would come to Round Dunes and spend the summer as Number One topic on the pool-to-beach grapevine. Now—joy unconfined—I care little for public opinion. Ellen in a bathing suit, fine!

I take her over to the Deutsches' apartment. "Present" her. The Deutsches aren't shy about asking questions. "Who are you attracted to," they asked, "men or women?" and Ellen, unflappable, says both. I'm pleased with how it goes, but afterward they challenge me.

"You said, 'I want you to see my sister!' " they tell me, and she said, "What am I, a carnival sideshow?" I'll have to take their word for it, as it lines up with earlier reports, namely with the way Patty and Lily thought I'd handled (or mishandled) their introduction to Ellen. My forcing her to talk about her experiences, and the differences between male and female physiognomy. So despite my best efforts to be casual, my deeper anxiety apparently manifests itself in what I say and how I say it. Being "open" and "unembarrassed" is my way of dealing with it, yet how much of a pose, a performance, is this? Later, with others—for example when someone asks me what I'm writing about—I can't just avoid answering, but instead of having a scripted answer ("a personal memoir about a family secret") I will drop it airily into the conversation ("My brother is now my sister!"), then rush on, my speed to get it over with a sort of preemptive defensive maneuver that doesn't fool anyone. And doesn't even discourage the questions I'm trying to avoid.

(I'm relieved when Ellen later tells me that, far from feeling I treated her as a freak, she was totally comfortable in both situations, that she'd never have said that about a carnival show except possibly as a joke, an icebreaker. "I know I'm a curiosity, probably the first transsexual most people have met, so it comes with the territory. It's true I want to blend in, but I also feel that the best thing I can do for transsexuals is to make the kind of good impression that might help their family and friends to accept and understand.")

Later during the Quogue visit, when Ellen is elsewhere, Nola, a keen analyst of human behavior and not one to keep her opinions to herself, asks me why Ellen wore such bright colors, the fuchsia lipstick, the turquoise jewelry, and why so blond? Is this Southern, she wants to know. Stephen was bothered by her muscular arms and "buff" look. Why would she wear sleeveless shirts? he wonders. I can't answer.

The next evening, the four of us are having dinner out. By this time we've gotten used to having Ellen among us. It's a festive occasion, very relaxed, and a wonderful break for me. At one point Nola says, "For siblings, you two are very different; you have very different interests and styles."

Ellen agrees readily. "Molly likes dark clothes," she says. "I guess it's a New York thing."

My heart leaps with relief, Ellen has liberated me. It wasn't just what she said, but the way she said it. There was clearly no envy or sense of inadequacy on her part. Not only does she *not* think her own way of dressing inferior, but she actually feels a little sorry for me in my drab urban ensembles and my less-is-more approach to makeup. This was what Stephen and Nola and I hadn't understood: that she liked and cultivated her own look, was proud of her body, buff, bright, a little shiny—and didn't want to hide it. In thinking of this, I'm suddenly reminded of my friend's reaction to the transsexual regarding herself with adoration in the store mirror. "Women never love their bodies like this," she said. I agreed at the time, but now I think it isn't—or isn't *quite*—that they love these bodies because they are *beautiful*, but because they are, finally, women's bodies.

In any case, from this moment on, I feel free to write about her taste and attire or anything else on which we might disagree. I've been sprung from some kind of shame or embarrassment, the need to treat her with kid gloves. I can't "hurt" her because she rejects the grounds on which my judgments might be formed. I might think of myself as a semistylish cosmopolitan New Yorker, but she has staked her ground as someone not particularly impressed by my taste and style. If I were condescending, the flaw, the failure of vision, would be in me rather than in her. She is not only my "equal" but my superior, for could I, in a similar situation, ever muster the confidence or self-acceptance she exudes?

Suddenly, it seems as if gender identity and its mutability is all anyone talks about. Women are playing "action heroes," men clueless schlubs who need to be coaxed out of adolescence. Transsexuals are celebrated in the novels of Jeffrey Eugenides and John Irving.

Strange things are going on in nature. In the Potomac River and its tributaries, in Virginia's Shenandoah River, male bass—so-called intersex fish—have been producing eggs. The high rate at which these fish are acquiring female sexual characteristics has raised concerns that pollutants might be causing the problem. In a scary bit of accelerated evolution, science writers note that the Y (male) chromosome is shrinking so rapidly that it could affect the activity of genes.

In the city, now without Ellen, I am on my own with Andrew. His memory has sprung gigantic leaks, his speech is hesitant, he has only one ear that can hear at all, he can barely walk, yet he manages to resume teaching in September. Far from making motions to remove him, Annette Insdorf, the valuable and indefatigable professor of film and onetime head of the film school, says they still want him at Columbia. He continues to be a draw for the film school—the last of the humanist-film scholars—and the students adore him, or at least seem willing to put up with his infirmities, but for how much longer? And he will need help just to get there and back.

In early October, I've planned to go for three weeks to VCCA, the writers' and artists' colony in Virginia, but have to cancel. Andrew is diagnosed with an aneurysm behind the knee and goes into Columbia-Presbyterian for surgery. I take over some of his classes as do other generous members of the teaching staff. While he is recovering in rehab, I go to visit Ellen. It's getting easier and easier to be with her. There's less of an inward shudder when I first see her, more pure pleasure.

I've never known anyone so orderly, and generally when I come, I have to review my checklist of what to do and what not to do. The kitchen is always pristine, as if unused, and the order extends even to the stacking of plates. There are eight and she rotates them from the dishwasher, latest washed on the bottom, so that one doesn't get used more than another. Put potholders under anything that comes out of the microwave; use the red chopping board for meat, the other for vegetables and fruit. Take off your shoes at the door. I use the guest bathroom and I'm instructed to leave the light on if I'm going in and out, as it uses more electricity, after a lifetime of being taught the opposite by conservation-minded citizens like my sibling. (It's about fluorescent versus incandescent.) The place is small, no storage, she has just what she needs and no more. Yet, I feel a little less constrained this time; I don't know if it's me or her.

I'm amazed not only at how many friends she seems to have but at how they come from all walks of life. She's on first-name, even confidential, terms with the Julie who's her manicurist, massage therapist, and also housekeeper; Toney, the man who was maintenence supervisor of some apartments she managed near the university; a woman tenant in the same complex who's suffered misfortunes on a biblical scale, and who, I suspect, is assisted by Ellen.

The best news is that there's also been a thawing of relations with Eleanor. She had decided to sell the Richmond house (hers in the settlement) and move to California to be near her daughter. Ellen had first seen her during the previous Christmas, when Eleanor casually said, Why don't you come on by.

Now in the summer of 2010 they've had to go through the arduous and heartbreaking process of emptying the house. In a notoriously bleak housing market, Eleanor sold it right away, so the job had to be accelerated. Ellen would come down often, sometimes there and back in the same day, carrying furniture or books or paintings that had to go to Pine Mountain. She and Eleanor never stopped working, sorting through their worldly possessions, packing boxes, dividing up, throwing out. Because the process was so hurried, they were losing track of what they'd sold, lost, kept. The relentless focus on work, Ellen told me later, kept the emotions under the surface. But as soon as the task was over, and the two sat lost in the empty house they'd put so much of themselves into, they broke down and cried. (Ellen still cries when she describes this scene.) But Eleanor could no longer keep Ellen at arm's length, and at least some of the sorrow was shared rather than recriminatory. And finally, she agreed to travel with Ellen. They're going to come to New York together in December to stay at Ellen's time-share unit.

It seems that time, so often a thief and a scourge, was on their side.

We talk about her social life now. One thing I wanted to know: What does it mean when you are a heterosexual woman? Do men "turn you on"? Are you sexually attracted, or is it just a matter of companionship?

"You always wonder. Not having had sex with a man, I can't really be sure other than I know that I'm attracted to them . . . but I can't get rid of my attraction to women. You're in this land where you think you feel a certain way, but there are so many cross feelings.

"I would really like to have a relationship with a man, more than just one date, in my lifetime, but if I don't, I'll be disappointed but not devastated. We all know women who are incomplete without a man. I'm at the other end. I love my women friends, love going out with men, especially taking trips together. I have no interest in getting married, but I do enjoy men. If I don't have a relationship, it would be fun to go out with two or three men, dating them casually, since they don't like to feel tied down. That's true of me, too, because I know how they are. Men have antennae out for women who are desperate for a man. If one developed into a relationship, fine, but I'm independent about so many things. I don't know where it comes from."

It looks like Ellen is more like Mother and me than those mythical other transsexuals or the typical male. She wants her independence, but she'd like a man: health, intelligence, and humor primary, sex secondary. Or—as I imagine it—a kind of virility more important than carnality.

"On the other hand," she continues, "the idea of going on a date terrifies me. What do you do, what do you talk about?" (I suggest her transsexualism might be an opener.)

"Adam said if you want to meet men, you're in the wrong place. And I wonder if I'm here deliberately, to protect myself from the possibility, the fear of rejection."

Lisa, the woman who colors Ellen's hair, is a lesbian, and they have long conversations about their respective lives and feelings. When Lisa told Ellen she actually preferred being alone in the evening, and didn't want some lover pestering her with questions, Ellen suggested that Lisa might actually want to be (or at least live like) a male, that perhaps she was a female-to-male transsexual, at least in spirit.

Lisa seemed to respond to this, even take pride in it. "How can you want to be a *woman*?" she asked dismissively. Ellen was taken aback, even hurt. After all she'd told her, didn't Lisa realize how happy she was, how full her life, as a woman?

"And besides," she said to me, "I don't think, and never have thought, that women are secondary."

CHAPTER THIRTEEN

The Year of the Transsexual

You are more and more authentic the more you look like someone you dreamed of being.

—Agrado, in Pedro Almodóvar's 1999 film *All About My Mother*

I am not a boy, not a girl, I am not gay, not straight, I am not a drag queen, not a transsexual—I am just me, Jackie.

—Jackie Curtis

*T*rend spotters are calling 2010 the "Year of the Transsexual." By this they mean the new empowerment of gender nonconformists like James Franco, Lady Gaga, Miss T Brazil, the gorgeous model. It's all very "downtown" and reminiscent of the seventies, as celebrities "flirt with the other side," enjoying—the old buzzwords—fluidity of gender, or as a *Times* reporter puts it, defining themselves "on a spectrum of gender rather than simply male or female." The singer-songwriter and deliriously shape-shifting performance artist Justin Vivian Bond wishes to be addressed with the gender-neutral and onomatopoeic "Mx." The anthem might be taken from *The Rocky Horror Picture Show*: "I'm just a sweet transvestite from Transsexual, Transylvania!"

On the other hand, far from these hip fashionistas, these slippery sexual icons, transsexuals are vilified, their rights questioned, their status equivocal. Transgender performers are all over the map—beautiful, comical, eerie, and fifty shades of camp. But for those who are neither glamorous nor performers—that is, most of the approximately 700,000 transgender people in the country—there are job losses, frustration (they can't afford surgery; take risky silicone treatments), assault, murder.

From the moment Chevey made his revelation, even during the edict against writing, I filed away news and culture reports on stories of Transgender, subset Transsexual. At first it was a trickle. There were hopeful signs. In San Francisco (where else?), Theresa Sparks, former sex toy executive, became the first male-to-female candidate to run for district supervisor. In Atlanta (more surprising), the Georgia Supreme Court ruled in favor of a transgender politician who opponents claimed had misled voters by running for office as a woman. In Richmond, on the steps of the capitol, the noble edifice designed by Thomas Jefferson, Robyn Deane came out as a transitioning woman. Deane, who as a man was married for seventeen years to the sister of Governor Robert McDonnell, chose this venue with the express political purpose of embarrassing her former in-law, a Republican opponent of gay and transgender rights.

The trickle became a flood tide. "The Nation's First Pregnant Father," screams a tabloid headline. A former beauty queen, artificially inseminated and now a man, appears pregnant on *Oprah* and four months later has a baby girl. The sexes blur: refinements in male beautification include men sporting guyliner and tights (a.k.a. "mantyhose").

A "Personal Love" column addresses the quandaries and confusions among the new multigendered, for instance, when one partner in a lesbian relationship becomes a man and the other, once proud and comfortable in her same-sex orientation, is forced to drastically (and perhaps unsuccessfully) reorient as a heterosexual. There's androgyny chic: the *Vanity Fair* cover "Patti Smith Meets Johnny Depp."

Paul Auster's *The Brooklyn Follies* features a beautiful Haitian transvestite named Rufus, employee of the rogue Harry, ex-con, homosexual, and rare-book dealer. His She is like the Platonic ideal of woman, with long legs and a chiseled face, the modern-day equivalent of the beautiful men-boys with whom Greek men consorted. What woman can achieve such androgynous perfection? The fashion industry shows its preference for the male body type by using as models hipless, breastless, anorexic females. A short entry in the *Week* magazine in 2011 says, "The most sought-after model of this year's London fashion shows was 19-year-old Andrej Pejic, a man who specializes in modeling women's clothes." But over the door of this glamorous party, there might as well be a warning sign: "Plain Women, Aging Women, Masculine Women Need Not Apply."

Citing the horrifying incident of a transsexual woman being brutally attacked and spit on by two teenage girls in a McDonald's restaurant in Baltimore County, Eliza Gray reports in the *New Republic* (Summer 2011), "Transgender people are some of the least protected, most persecuted people in the United States."

Certainly we are a long way from the shock of Christine Jorgensen and Renée Richards, or those years mentioned by Candy Darling in a recent documentary when being a female impersonator on the streets of New York was against the law; or 1951, when Ernest Hemingway's son Gigi was arrested in a Los Angeles movie theater for entering the ladies' room dressed as a woman. But if Ellen is any example, far from exulting in their "equivocal" state, most transsexuals still tremble each time they enter a public restroom.

In the early days of transgender exploration, thanks to Harry Benjamin's pioneering work, gays, lesbians, and bisexuals, also subject to enormous discrimination, made common cause with transsexuals. But in the seventies there was a backlash, and they closed ranks against them—a bias that Susan Stryker (*Transgender History*) says has been somewhat repaired but "has yet to be fully overcome."

There are movies extremely sympathetic to transsexuals, like João Pedro Rodrigues's *To Die Like a Man*, a poignant and melancholy fable about the life and death of a drag queen. Harking back to Fassbinder's tragic *In a Year of 13 Moons*, Rodrigues's much warmer film shows us so many states of joy and sorrow as to make any kind of stereotyping impossible. Kimberly Reed, once a quarterback at her Midwestern high school, now a beautiful she-editor in New York, has made a fascinating documentary, *Prodigal Sons*, about her own transsexualism. In it, this onetime high-school jock returns to a welcoming class reunion. "Well, everybody changes," says one of her unperturbed former classmates.

More controversial was the burlesque *Ticked-Off Trannies with Knives*, shown at the Tribeca Film Festival, which aroused the hackles of GLAAD (the Gay and Lesbian Alliance Against Defamation), who protested Israel Luna's film as a misrepresentation of transgender women.

GLAAD was again outraged by a very funny *Saturday Night Live* skit purporting to advertise an estrogen supplement, Estro Maxx, which, taken daily, turns a guy with a mustache into a girl. So successful was their protest that when I sent the link to Ellen to get her opinion, it had already been "removed by the user."

I asked her what she thought of that. In my view, the more transsexuals are *out there*, in whatever form, the sooner the public becomes habituated. But what does Ellen think?

"I don't have a strong reaction. Mostly, I'd say, what a wuss to put yourself out there as cutting edge but the minute somebody jumps on you, you take it down. The time to take it down is before you air it in the first place. Once it gets vetted, put your name on it, stand by it. It's true of everybody that you might say something off the cuff, then be sorry and apologize. But a skit is not something done quickly. Of course, it's bowing to advertisers so I'm really talking to the advertisers. But if you put money in *SNL* you're going to offend people; that's the whole show.

"My real resentment is against gays who don't want anything to do with us. They're a protected class now and we're not."

That's not entirely true anymore. Though legal protection for transsexuals is basically ten or fifteen years behind the legalization of gay rights, increasingly states and other jurisdictions have added language to include transgender nondiscrimination. The Transgender Civil Rights Project, part of the National Gay and Lesbian Task Force, tracks various forms of discrimination worldwide; although we in the United States have miles to go in both legal protection and public attitudes, conditions in other parts of the world—particularly Asia and Latin America—are far worse. More shocking than the prohibitions in these traditional societies is a law in Sweden and sixteen other European countries (including France and Italy) that forces would-be transsexuals to be sterilized.*

I talk to Dr. Jack Drescher, eminent psychiatrist and an authority on gay and transgender issues. "It's supposed to protect the 20 percent who have regrets," he says, "but in effect, it punishes the 80 percent who don't. They have to go through a whole other set of hoops." Drescher was part of the American Psychiatric Association's task team that recently updated the important *Diagnostic and Statistical Manual*, and notes that the decision to remove transsexualism from the "disorder" category (as homosexuality was removed in 1973) has caused a

---

* Thanks to a groundswell of opposition, the Swedish parliament changed this law early in 2013.

rift between those who appreciate the destigmatization and others who fear it could lead to a loss of medical insurance. I ask whether the decision of some states, like California, to offer coverage for surgery for its citizens could lead to problems, like transsexual candidates flooding the state, or a public backlash against them.

"There really shouldn't be a problem," he says. "Transsexuals are such a tiny minority, but they've been blown up, sensationalized through television, out of all proportion to the actual numbers."

There have been various antidiscrimination bills, largely for state employees, and New York pioneered legal name change, becoming, as one reporter put it, the "capital of 'Joe-to-Jane' proceedings," with a whole phalanx of lawyers devoted to the legal intricacies of name change.

New York also moved to allow transsexuals to change their birth certificates so as to reflect their new identity, an option that many transsexuals have embraced but that I find almost more troubling than anything else. For those who do insist they were always the sex they have become, what about the lives they lived with others—as, say, husband and father, daughter or wife? Here we get to the core of that overused and amorphous word, "identity." Is our subjective sense of ourselves the only authority on who we are and were? Have we the right to annul the past; does it belong only to us? Undoubtedly this revisionism on the part of transsexuals springs from a hunger for recognition, and perhaps if they make the change earlier there will be less need to rewrite history. But aren't we all a composite of selves formed and reflected in our encounters with others, our relationships, and our pasts, awkwardness and alienation included? There may be a very real difference between those who felt the "wrongness" of their sexual identity very early on (at two or three or four) and those who came into an awareness of it later, but I still can't accept such a willful erasure of the past, and luckily Ellen has no wish to do so.

"I don't deny my male side," she says, "I cherish it. This turns out to have a huge impact on every aspect of my life."

It's December. Ellen and I discuss Christmas presents. I suggest a tennis warm-up suit. She likes the idea, so while on the phone, we go online to window-shop. We're discussing her size, the difference between bottom and top, broad shoulders and narrow hips, so I suggest a man's outfit and point out a few. Nothing doing. They're all too drab and neutral; she chooses a bright blue woman's suit with feminine details.

Later in the month, she arrives with Eleanor as planned, and I meet them for lunch at the Boathouse.

Afterward, the three of us come back to the apartment to see Andrew. Only one gaffe on my part. Andrew's teaching assistant Jonathan happens to be on the same elevator coming up. I have to introduce them and it comes out, "This is my sister and her ex-wife." There would have been better ways to do it, but they're always either euphemistic or incomplete. Not the least hurdle in the journey of transsexuals and their families is the awkwardness of introductions and the problem of pronouns. Language simply hasn't evolved to keep pace with such complex relationships.

Andrew's delighted to see them, and Eleanor is surprised at how much his old self Andrew is. As we laugh I mourn the good times we all had together, the trips the four of us will never take again.

After their visit, I call Eleanor. She knows I'm writing the book and, as much as she dreads the exposure, she understands how and why I must do it, and perhaps even welcomes the chance to give her perspective. We go back over the past few years, and the day Chevey as Ellen appeared on her doorstep.

"I remember it so well. I was sitting at the desk and she came in and sat in an armchair. I can see the humor in it now. She was like a little girl in an Easter outfit. She tucked her feet under her, placed her hands close together on her lap, as if asking, 'Mommy, don't I look pretty?' As I told you I broke down. I don't think it was the reaction she was expecting.

"She had a very vivid fantasy life," Eleanor continues, "imagining dressing as a woman. I think sometimes she bought things for me, told me how becoming they were, but wasn't thinking about me at all, just about how they might look on her if she were a woman.

"Now I think: I was really duped. I was living a lie but didn't know it. Once I started looking back, my life came crumbling down like a house of cards. He was living vicariously through me.

"One of the hardest things of all is when I see Ellen now doing things John wouldn't do. Now I see her making friends, being popular. I think of all the things I gave up, and her life is taking off with all those things we didn't get to do.

"She wants things to be as they were, but they can never be the way they were. That's all gone. I still have the memory and the history, but I don't feel about her as I did. It's hard to be around her for extended periods of time. And it's easier to be together in private than in public."

There is in this story of transformation no such thing as an unqualified triumph.

Most of the beginning of 2011 I seem to spend on Andrew, managing his retirement and worrying over a constantly proliferating string of details, financial, legal, and medical, looking into caretaking possibilities.

It is now the end of May and I'm finally going to have my three-week stint at VCCA, the writers and artists colony in the mountains of

Virginia. I hold my breath, praying that some emergency doesn't inter-vene, that Andrew won't fall or deteriorate radically. At present, he is mentally and physically unsteady, and has someone with him four or five hours a day, preparing his meals, getting him ready for bed. But he can still go by himself on his walker to the rehab clinic a block away.

I'll go down by train and Ellen, who lives not far away, will come for the day after I'm settled and into my work. The very air is filled with ghosts and demons since the retreat happens to be just across the high-way from the women's college I attended. When I wake up in the morn-ing, it's madeleine time in Virginia. The intense, hot hum of the balmy air plunges me back into the summers of my childhood, and various versions of myself bump and collide. Surrounded by like-minded fel-lows, the working writer hits the ground running, but, suddenly, I can't sleep. Night after night. I talk to Andrew often, but I'm torn between the liberation of work and a mind uneasy for my beloved.

I knew if I was ever going to write this book, I had to get away. He knew it, too, and completely supported the venture. But now that I am "free," I'm not. My life has revolved around Andrew for so long, and, stressful as that has been, the Jane Eyre role of caretaker devoting one-self to a dependent husband, has the satisfaction of removing "selfish-ness" from the table. The demons of guilt, ever on the alert for a pretext to pounce, have lain dormant. No longer. I have been sprung from the obligations that had filled my days and it has opened the floodgates to the unconscious.

Nightmare follows nightmare. My husband and I talk several times a day, and despite his support, he keeps asking, pleading, When are you coming home? He loses track of time, and I try to reassure him. One night I dream that I arrive at our apartment on Eighty-Eighth Street to find some sort of saturnalia under way. Andrew is standing on the land-ing of a staircase (it isn't quite our apartment, rather an eerie combination of loft and grand salon), while all around him strange revelers are drinking, laughing, merrymaking. And Andrew, thin and taller than he is now, is wearing a *dress*, a glittery sheath affair. I am devastated. *Et tu*, Andrew! He is *also* becoming a woman. Both my men becoming women. And he has no idea who these people are, or why they are there. They are taking advantage of him, probably stealing (my fears of the trustworthiness of the various caretakers I've hired), so I immediately take charge: "Thank you all for coming," I say in a commanding voice, "and now please leave." I wake up shaking, nauseated. In the telling it sounds amusingly ironic, but it didn't play that way. The feeling of abandonment and betrayal is unendurable, worse than if he'd died. I lie there in a cold sweat, the dream still clinging to me, feeling I've lost Andrew as I knew him. It's like that falling-into-the-abyss moment that comes, probably must come, in all long relationships, when you look at the person you love and for a terrifying instant you don't love him anymore. The terror that envelops you arises from the fact that if *he* is a stranger—as he is at this moment—so are *you*. A stranger to yourself, instead of the familiar being that fits into this other familiar being like a hand in a glove. The ground shifts beneath you; as Othello says, "When I love thee not, chaos is come again."

Later, with coffee and a full awakening, I get some distance from the dream, and the aesthete in me can't help but appreciate its mythic resonance. Odysseus returning to Penelope to find her surrounded by swilling suitors. And the obvious and painful role reversal: I am now the "man," the protector, and Andrew, in his dependency, the woman.

And that feels bloody awful. This isn't the role reversal I celebrate as a film critic and lecturer. This isn't the cute, caustic back-and-forth of Katharine Hepburn and Spencer Tracy in *Adam's Rib*, and the other charming cutups of screwball comedy, nor is it the deliciously sinister death struggle between masochistic men and spider-dames in film noir. This is the role reversal of aging and it goes in only one direction.

And then I think, this dream, this nightmare, is a gift. In one of those astonishing feats of integration and expansion that dreams perform, Andrew's "feminization" brings Ellen's epic migration from male to female, seemingly so weird and exceptional, much closer to home, hits me where I live in every sense of the word. The transsexual plays out, in a more sensational form, humankind's drama of transformation, the androgyny of aging, the overlapping and reconfiguring of roles as we cope with an ever-changing array of new opportunities, but also new disabilities. And suddenly I know, on another, deeper level, why I have to write this book. It isn't just about Ellen, it's about me. And Andrew. And everyone I know.

Ellen comes over for a day visit. I show her around and introduce her to several fellows. We go out for lunch, after which she comes back and solves whatever computer problems I'm having. Then she catches me up with her latest "T" adventures.

"I was taking the train from New York to Philadelphia; it was very crowded and a woman sat next to me. We read, chatted, read some more. When a seat became available by a window, the woman moved over. She was having a very hard time getting her suitcase up on the rack. She struggled and struggled. I thought maybe it wouldn't fit. 'Want me to try it?' I asked. The woman nodded."

"Did you put on a show of making it difficult?" I ask.

"Not quite enough apparently. She thanked me, and said, 'Wow, I've got to go to the gym more often.'"

But the kicker came when they got to Philadelphia.

"Do you want me to help you with your bag?" Ellen asked. "No," the woman replied, "I have a man to do that."

CHAPTER FOURTEEN

Ellen Is a Medicare Mudder

The wood that finds itself a violin . . .
—Rimbaud

*I*t's a mild Monday in October, and later in the day I'll fly down for a much-anticipated visit with Ellen. For the moment I'm in the waiting room of a doctor's office, for follow-up surgery on a minor skin cancer. In the waiting room I come across a woman I know, a composer, whose husband is here, like me, for follow-up. While he's having his stitches removed, the two of us chat. I glance at my watch, telling her I have to catch a plane to visit my sister, and we talk about the mountains where she lives. Later in the conversation, she mentions taking the car-train to Florida. I tell her I used to go there when my mother had an apartment in Delray, but she gave it to my brother as part of his inheritance, and he sold it. "I hope he got a good price for it," she says, thinking of the dismal housing market in Florida. But all I can think of is: she thinks I have a brother *and* a sister. Not that it matters to her, but still. Two siblings. Well, if we think of them as successive rather than simultaneous, I guess I do. You're never quite free of these conversational conundrums.

I've planned this visit to Pine Mountain to see Ellen and enjoy the splendor of autumn foliage, but also to meet and interview some of her friends. We settled on Monday because the weekend was taken over by an outdoor event called, appropriately and dauntingly, the "Tough Mudder." Ellen has told me about this hair-raising physical trial, not a competition exactly (everyone cooperates), but a grueling obstacle course that takes place in various rugged terrains around the United States. This is the first time they've held it at Pine Mountain, and thousands of participants, both men and women, will have come from all over to submit to such athletic ordeals and indignities as wading through freezing water, climbing up and down mountains, scaling high walls, passing through electric cattle-jolt wires. Ellen and her friends had planned to watch and supply water from the sidelines. After she picks me up at the airport and we're driving up the mountain, I ask her how it went. She describes all the gory details—the trials are meant to be both mentally and physically punishing—and it sounds like sheer masochism. "Who on earth would want to *do* that?" I ask.

A slight smile comes to Ellen's face. "I did it," she says.

I'm stunned but (unlike her friends on the mountain, as I'll discover) not completely surprised. The way she did it was pure Ellen, both reckless and cautious. It was, she tells me, no hasty decision. Although she'd applied early (even securing permission to have a T-shirt that read: "Medicare Mudder"), she hadn't decided to actually enter until the night before. She adds that, as her hairdresser told her mud could ruin her hair color, she avoided those obstacles in which she might get immersed. And she refused to do one that entailed jumping straight down onto a surface so hard it could have twisted an ankle or even the spine (it was the only one about which many participants complained afterward). She always worries that if something happens to her she'll be in the apartment alone, with no one to help. And suppose she broke or sprained something on the eve of my visit. She had to have been the oldest person in the event; most were in their twenties and thirties. But the temptation, the challenge, was too much, and the success clearly exhilarating. That's Ellen, I thought.

She'd hoped to pass unnoticed by her friends at Pine Mountain, but those who lined the course supplying water and snacks quickly relayed reports, so that by the time I got there, the whole mountaintop—or the fairly large year-round group who knew Ellen—was abuzz with the news.

"We didn't think she'd do anything to muss up her hair!" laughs Liz, the young, recently married administrator at the Nature Foundation and my first "interview." She's also the organizer and leader of well-reviewed trips to such places as Banff and hiking trips in Canada. Like everyone at Pine Mountain, she has only known Ellen as Ellen.

"She is so much a lady," Liz continues, "prissy, hilarious, Southern; I can't even imagine her as a man. The coolest person ever, way more of a chick than I will ever be.

"I also think she's one of the strongest people I've ever met. I watch her interact with people and they adore her. If she ever chose to leave Pine Mountain, it would be one of the biggest losses, especially to the Nature Foundation. She gives her heart and soul for us. If we have an event we always wait with bated breath, hoping Ellen will come.

"This place is both conservative and open. She disarmed everyone with her honesty, the way she approached the Mountain Women. She never tried to present herself as anything other than what she was."

"But there must have been ticklish situations . . . ?"

"Yes, we were very protective of her, especially the first year or two; we came to her defense in situations with people she didn't know. Then we realized we didn't have to. She's very funny, she's fine on her own."

The surprise over Tough Mudder was not restricted to the hair issue. There was also her age. A lot of the men were intimidated, thinking if *she* can do it, I can and should. Everyone teased her, demanding ocular proof, something more than the headband provided those who finished the race. So pictures were e-mailed to everyone, showing an Ellen triumphant but suitably bedraggled.

I'm nonplussed by one reaction to Ellen that seems universal among her coterie at Pine Mountain. They see her as a quintessential Richmond lady. Refined. Genteel. Outgoing, charming. Always made-up and well dressed (that may be, but certainly not in the conservative style of Richmond, which inclines toward the "classic"—moderately expensive suits and dresses that are of durable fabric and "never go out of style"). This strikes me as funny in ways I can't begin to count. Mainly, what would they say in West End Richmond if they knew that somewhere not so far away, they were being represented by a transsexual! Maybe all those miles clocked at cotillion and debutante parties have paid off, giving Ellen the confidence and "social skills" required. After all, dancing requires an attunement to the other person.

For the people of Pine Mountain, who've been all over the world, but probably not to Richmond, the "Southern Lady" is an archetype, a social myth, which Ellen embodies. If she's not completely convincing as a female (the voice; the size), her portrayal of the "Richmond lady" is Oscar-worthy.

But this view, expressed by everyone I talk to, also brings home to me the disjunction between the way others see us and the way we see ourselves. I talk to Ellen about it. Neither of us thinks of herself that way. Richmond lady certainly never occurs to me as a definition of myself. For I assume that although I still bear remnants of my upbringing, I came to New York to avoid being (just) a Richmond lady, or someone who is primarily thought of as such. It's not a rejection of Richmond, just a marginalization of it in my psyche, a desire to escape the constraints of decorousness. Yet, I'm sure it's high on the list of traits by which others perceive me.

With Ellen it's slightly different. Her ladyhood is hard-won, requires constant vigilance and application. The women of Pine Mountain laugh and tease her about always being "perfect," saying they dress like slobs while she always has on lipstick, earrings, and is well dressed, putting them all to shame. Many of them are of an age, and at a place, where they can thankfully shrug off such concerns, care less and do less about clothes and makeup. But Ellen brings them up short. She reminds me, "I don't just do it because I'm so 'feminine,' but because it's dangerous not to. They sometimes forget that I always have to worry about slurs or worse, about an attack in a public place. It could be a matter of life and death, therefore I have to do everything I can to be a convincing woman. I am getting more relaxed about it now, at least on the mountaintop. Four years ago I would have put on lipstick and fixed my hair to carry the garbage out and sweep the snow off my car. Today I slipped on some hiking pants to cover my pajama legs, put a heavy coat on over my pajama top, pulled the hood over my head, and out I went. No lipstick, no nothing. Admittedly, I was pretty covered up. But I guess that means I've 'arrived'!"

Sue, the lovely, warm, and adventurous woman and free spirit I'd met in New York, says she first knew about Ellen through Mountain Women. Her reaction, when told of Ellen's request to join the group, was simple curiosity.

"I immediately went on the Web to find out about transgender. I'd seen something in Japan, a *Cage aux Folles*–type of revue, with all males dressed as women. I noticed them all looking at me—I was the only blond in a sea of Asians. Afterward, someone asked me if I'd like to come backstage and meet them, and I said yes. I got to talking to one—they were mostly males planning on having surgery to become females—and asked why they'd focused on me. 'Oh,' she said, 'we were so afraid of offending you!'

"Ellen was so open," says Sue, "so gracious, and she had such a sense of humor, that I found myself quite charmed by her, and more and more open to her condition. As did all the Mountain Women.

"We all travelled together, were comfortable with her, and she won everybody over. She was clearly raised in a family that valued good manners. Another thing is that she never put her issues on us. Many do. They're hurt and angry and confused. And their anger spills over. This happened in the women's movement, with the confusion about roles in the seventies and eighties. I didn't sense that in Ellen. She's older, more mature, and had led a successful life as a man, which perhaps made a difference. There was no chip on her shoulder but instead that Richmond gentility, plus her own personality, open and patient. She won the community over. I never heard anything against her either up on the mountain or from the women in the valley. And she's one of the most courageous people I've ever seen.

"Also, I think this may be why it's been so hard on her wife—to have to leave someone so loving. No one walks out on a good provider, either. It's much easier to divorce if the husband is bad."

We talk about how we occasionally get mixed up about our roles. Sue says Ellen always opens the door for her. "She does the guy thing—driving a sports car, lifting heavy bags. Her gallantry combined with her empathy. It's like having a girlfriend and a boyfriend." Sue pauses. "If I'd known her as a guy, I could have fallen in love with her."

She agrees as to Ellen's impeccable presentation. "She takes such joy in being female, so much more than those of us born that way. The rest of us are retired, run around looking like death warmed over, without makeup. But she gets up and gets dressed, always beautifully, loves jewelry and makeup. It's why we were all so shocked at Ellen doing the Tough Mudder. For instance, her makeup. The rest of us went through all that in high school, trying different looks, learning to use makeup. She never looks like a slob. She'll ask me to look at an outfit she's just bought, and it's fun having a woman friend who enjoys all that."

I ask her about Ellen's effect, or impact, on others, since it's one thing I'm blind to.

"Here, she's in a safe place, but she's very tall, and she almost expects people to figure it out, 'read' her. I think she's especially afraid of men in groups. That's a lot of stress. And then there's ladies' rooms, where she won't talk at all.

"When she first came to me and said she wanted to work at the Nature Foundation, I told her, if the foundation leadership is comfortable with you, then do it. She worried about taking people on hikes, especially children.

"But why this anxiety about children!" Sue explodes. "When Chaz was on *Dancing with the Stars*, some women's group complained, 'How do we explain it to children?' Why explain it to children! He's Chaz and he's dancing with the stars."

I could only applaud her wisdom. We agree that when it comes to sexual issues, children filter them out or register them only when they're ready.

Ellen has such a lot of friends; I ask her about the social life Chevey had—or didn't have—with Eleanor.

"We didn't have one but that's just the way our marriage was. We saw a lot of her relatives, but Eleanor's friends, her whole social life, were centered on the church and Sunday school, and mostly they were all women. I'd promised when we married to go to church occasionally, and I did, and to special occasions, but the women and their husbands never came to our place. She never said anything about wanting people over."

"But you were never exactly Mr. Party Animal when you were married to Beth."

"True, though she was more of a hermit than I was. I always liked a moderate amount of social life, but up here it's nonstop. Of course we're like pioneers in a one-horse town and the next settlement is miles away. But it's true: whether because of hormones, or being re-tired, or getting older and more relaxed, I enjoy being with people; I even enjoy writing thank-you notes!"

We're sitting in her apartment, and now her transsexualism is no longer the central fact of our lives—it either comes up or it doesn't. We're both trying to open a tightly sealed bag of chips by pulling out the two sides (so it can vacuum-close more easily) and having a hard time of it. "We need a man," she says. And she tells me about an inci-dent at the supermarket, emblematic of many others. She arrived at the checkout line and the cashier, eyeing her three heavy bags, says, "Don't you need someone to help you with that?" Ellen thought about the hassle involved in the "female" option—waiting for someone to come and fill a cart, take it out to the car, load up the trunk, etc., as opposed to her carrying it all herself and potentially giving herself away with the manly show of strength.

"I'll just take it," she says.

"Now I know that the people who knew me before—understand-ably—have a much harder time with this. It's like they are witnessing someone close to them who died and then came back in a different body. It's almost like some 1950s science-fiction movie: *Mabel, don't you recognize me? Just because I look like a gigantic ant? It's Fred! Don't you recognize me?* And I feel this way, but it's not really funny in real life. It's tragic. As I said before, the sorrow you inflict on others you can never get away from.

"I haven't really had any bad reactions here. I'm sure they're talk-ing behind my back, although I sense it's probably nowhere near as bad as I once thought or some people once thought. I think that prob-ably the truer thing is that they're just not talking about me at all. I was a somewhat restrained male—I don't want to say conservative because that has more negative connotations. I was reserved. I'm the same as a female. Nothing changed. I was an identical twin, but it's like twins who are so similar in many ways, but they each have their own differences. I'm just the other half now."

Some friends have dropped away. I ask about Karl, the buddy with whom he went to gun shows. Chevey waited for the occasion and told him about his plans, and Karl seemed to take it in stride. It was only later that Karl admitted that he'd pulled over to the side of the road and had a meltdown. And now he's sort of disappeared.

On the other hand, Toney, the maintenance supervisor from the pre-Ellen past, has been a supporter and made a real discovery relating to the voice problem.

"At first, when it started dropping during a conversation, Toney would say, 'Voice.' It worked, but it always threw me off whatever I was talking about. Then he came up with a signal, thumbs-up. He does that now, my voice rises a register, and somehow the brain doesn't get sidetracked."

She's delirious when someone fails to "read" her and tells me about an incident when she was at a benefit dinner for the foundation. First of all, she was invited to replace someone who had cancelled.

"They didn't need to call me," she said, "I would never have known the difference. And that has happened over and over again.

"I sat next to a woman I didn't know, and we hit it off. We talked to other people at the table, but she and I kept talking. It was a relaxed setting in a beautiful home, we were all laughing and carrying on, and then it emerged that this very laid-back woman practices law in three different countries. That's very characteristic of the people here—very casual, then you find out they are retired admirals or diplomats.

"Then an hour into the party, she asked me about my past and I mentioned that when I got out of college back in the late sixties I went to Wheat and Company as a stockbroker. She knew of the company and said, 'You must have been the first woman stockbroker there.' And of course I glowed. It had been a long day, I felt tired and my voice wasn't doing very well, and I just said, 'You don't know how good that makes me feel.' And I explained why."

There's a cocktail party to introduce me to her friends, and I'm impressed by their cosmopolitanism. One's an ex-professor, another a woman in real estate, still another a Frenchman who loves Virginia.

I meet Cindy, one-half of a couple who are sort of Pine Mountain's First Family, perched on the uppermost aerie of the mountains, respected by all. Cindy's husband, John, who's agreed to speak with me the following day, is in Omaha—he's a consultant in what's called corporate citizenship, advising companies on how to carry out charity and philanthropy, whether or not they should start a foundation. He turns out to be, like Cindy, open, genial, intelligent.

"Pine Mountain is not a microcosm of the world," he reminds me. "It's good for Ellen. It's not cliquey. I'm a golfer and skier but also interested in the Nature Foundation. We full-timers are mostly retired, fairly smart, open-minded, a good mix. There's a jock contingent, maybe a little more conservative. The Nature Foundation where she spends so much time is more liberal, not all tree huggers; a lot of them like to ski.

"The real issue is understanding. A golf friend of mine met Ellen and the next time we were playing he told me he met this new woman, and when they shook hands, they were the biggest hands of any woman he'd ever met. I told him she used to be a he. 'Oh, gay?' he asked. 'No.' 'A cross-dresser?' 'No, physically changed,' I told him. 'How in the hell do you do that?' he asked. I think I finally made him understand that it was not just surgery, it was hormones, it was a whole kind of life change. It was an education. Most men are thrown by it because they can't understand how or why anyone would . . ." (He decorously omits the obvious.)

John feels the Christian conservatives have it all wrong in thinking that people can be seduced into being gay, transsexual, whatever. The daughter of one of their friends was a compulsive cutter, but when she was hospitalized, and had some biopsies done, they found a growth in the brain, and she was treated successfully.

I learn more of the mental divide between the present company, who live on the mountain, and Pine Mountain's other community, down in the valley. Like two tribes in ancient Greece, they regard each other with mutual incomprehension. The mountaineers, who are definitely closer to Spartans than the valley is to Athenians, look down on the softies, wondering why they would live in those little plots with neither views nor amenities, a sort of suburb without an urb. The valley people can't imagine living on the mountain, where it's always ten or more degrees colder, fine in the summer, but summer is short compared to those long winters when residents are often marooned by snow, icy mountain roads, electrical shortages, a rugged life.

Chevey always loved mountains, from the time we spent summers as children in High Hampton in North Carolina. I, too, loved High Hampton and went to camp in the mountains of North Carolina. But I'm a fair-weather friend. I hate the cold, not to mention wind and fog. Ellen's apartment, 3,500 feet above sea level, is sometimes in the clouds. We'll wake up, unable to see a tree forty feet away, while it's sunny down in the valley. The mist will sometimes hover all day. But whatever the weather, she enjoys sitting by the window, drinking her coffee, communing with what's there and what's not there. I may not love the mountains, but I begin to understand something of the bond these people share, a love of nature that overrides class, gender, origins. They're adventurous without being compulsive or self-congratulatory (or maybe just a bit, in contrast to the soft mudders below).

I look at the plants again and realize that many I had previously classed as artificial—the African violets, the ivy—are in fact real. I notice things I hadn't noticed before: the exquisitely handmade honeysuckle to which is attached a paper caterpillar one inch long, and the green-red hummingbird, made of wood, held to a blossom by the tiny end of his beak.

CHAPTER FIFTEEN

Looking Backward and Moving Forward

"*R*emember that fear I told you about," our conversation continues, "that I'd be in the Village shopping center and some little girl would come with her mother and say, 'Why is that man dressed like a woman?' It finally came true," says Ellen with a laugh. "I was volunteering at the Nature Foundation, where I stand behind the desk and man (well, *woman*) the cash register, gift shop, and give advice. It was a busy morning, your voice gets tired, you're tired, not doing your best job. There were two young women, asking about hikes; I was showing them the map and explaining. They had one or two children, one listened beside her mom and right in the middle—we're talking about different trails—the girl pipes up and says, 'Are you a man wearing lipstick?'

"I gasped inwardly, thought a minute, and said, 'No, I'm a woman, but I used to be a man.' The little girl went off to look at something else.

"Her mother looked at me and said, 'You handled that very well.' When you're tired, things slip. It was bound to happen sooner or later, and I'm glad I got it behind me.

"Remember how I told you that when I go into a ladies' room with friends, I don't talk? If I'm in a stall and someone hears my voice, it might cause a panic. I have visions of police waiting for me when I come out. But if people just see me I've got a pretty good chance of passing. When I'm on the phone—that's when I always get 'Yes, sir.' I call to make a reservation, I say, 'It's Ellen Hampton, E-L-L-E-N,' and it's 'Yes, sir, how may I help you?'

"There are times now when I'll be at a social gathering or a meeting and a man will put his arm on my back or hand on my shoulder, or grab my hand and hold it longer than normal, and it sends a delicious electric shock through me, like a lightning bolt. It doesn't necessarily mean anything, but my imagination runs wild. Don't tell me anything important for the next thirty minutes, because I won't take it in."

Has there been anything like a hit or a flirtation? I ask her.

"One day I was volunteering for the Nature Foundation block party, a barbecue, so I'd get to know people. I was hosting a card table, signing people in, giving them a name tag. There was a long line, and people would arrive at the table one by one. It was another of those times when I was tired, frantic, and forgot about the voice. This guy, a hippie type with a ponytail and camouflage pants, arrived at my table, and was filling out a form. Then he crouched down near the card table and the next thing he says is, 'I love your deep voice.'

" 'Oh, I'm trying to raise it,' I said. But he went on and on. He got his application, then he came back again and again. The woman next to me was having a ball. 'He's looking at you,' she'd say, then, 'He's hit on you again.' I was getting more and more irritated, but I was trapped: I represented the Nature Foundation and couldn't just leave. By the end of the evening, as soon as the time was up, I scurried out the back door.

"Another time I was coming into my apartment. It was November, a cool evening. I'd been hiking. I was in old clothes and bringing in firewood from the outdoor pile. As I walked in, a man came out, a guy in his forties, in bicycle clothes, fairly bright and distinctive. I go in, put the firewood down, go back for another load, and pass him a second time.

"The next day, I had business to do in town. I came home, laid the fire, and was getting ready to have a bit of dinner, when there was a knock on the door. I asked who's there and it was—I'll call him 'Jack'; he was renting one of the apartments in the building. He'd brought some firewood for me, so I had him put it down by the fire and made a quick decision. He was good-looking, a real hunk. I invited him to have a drink. For three hours we had a wonderful evening, talking, laughing. While he was there, there was no problem with the voice. It wasn't great but I kept the pitch up. It turned out Jack was actually fifty years old, an extreme athlete who did marathons, mountain cycling, had his own company, a girlfriend in the town where he came from. He would stop the conversation and pay me a really nice compliment, saying how beautiful I was, something specific about my looks.

"About an hour into it, he said, 'I can't believe, as good-looking as you are, any man would ever divorce you or let you divorce him.' As I've said, I don't get into the fact that I'm a 'T' unless it's somebody I think I'll have a relationship with, and most of the times not even then, only when the conversation seems to require it, and if the subject can slide in easily.

"I paused for a long time, thinking he's really put me on the spot. How to answer? So I told him the truth. I thought that he'd found me attractive enough after the previous night, that maybe he was just after easy sex. Which I actually found a morale booster. And the fact that I'd gone for an hour or more without blowing it.

"He said something like 'I wondered about that,' but I don't really think he had. It was a nervous reaction; he was caught by surprise. It turns out he has two grown sons, and he's a little unsure about the sexual orientation of the one in college. If it's true, the boy is probably scared to death of his dad finding out anything. He's a nice, gentle guy but also very macho. He doesn't act it but he looks it, with the bulging muscles.

"I tell him at the end, 'Have a conversation with your son, tell him about the wonderful evening you had with a transsexual; that will let him know you're not going to kill him if he's gay.'

"As he left, he gave me a great big hug. It was wonderful—a real validation."

She seems more relaxed in every way this time. It seems to me there is great joy in Ellen's life, some of it from her relationship with the natural world around her. She takes people on hikes, thus knows a lot of history of the landscape she loves. She's one of those rare people who's in tune with the beauty of what William James called "the secret life of nature," acknowledging (in the short book *Blindness*) a blind spot that most of us share.

She tells me about an outing she took with some of the Mountain Women. They were sitting around having dinner and wine, and one of them said, "Why don't men do this? I'm always saying to my husband, 'Why don't you go out with your buddies and have a beer?' But they never do."

It's because that's the way men are, Ellen told the group. It's the same in the animal kingdom. The women congregate but the males— the lions, the tigers—are loners. Too competitive to join together. It's the way evolution has designed us.

"I know both feelings as I've been both. Now my social side is stronger, but I have my solitary side, too. But for my women friends, I'm a sort of consultant on how men think. Sometimes I think I've been very lucky. I'd never have thought that way starting out, but here I am—being both genders in the same lifetime. Some people might even be jealous."

When next I talk to Eleanor, I tell her I understand her resentments but can't agree that Chevey was ever doing things just for himself. Yes, as he's acknowledged, he often bought presents for both wives he'd have liked for the imaginary "Ellen," but never *just* for that: he loved Eleanor too much, was too considerate a person, wanted to give her pleasure in dress, in lovemaking.

"I know," she sighs. "He was very attentive and caring. He walked into a situation where the children weren't his and was more like a real father. I have to stop going back and second-guessing everything that ever happened. I have to honor the memories that were there for what they were and not readdress and rearrange them as they appear according to the present situation."

I talk to Ellen, having just watched the HBO movie *Normal* (2003), with Jessica Lange and Tom Wilkinson. The beginning is unpromising, replete with dumbed-down stereotypes and implausibilities: they're a good (i.e., clueless) Baptist family in farm country, celebrating their twenty-fifth wedding anniversary, when Wilkinson keels over. The big galoot is really a woman and can't endure being a man any longer. What follows is sad, funny, grotesque, sometimes straining credulity—at one point Wilkinson, who works in a farm machinery plant, walks into the locker room wearing earrings, whereupon his macho coworkers predictably attack him. But the movement toward acceptance on the part of the family is deeply moving, especially the manner in which Lange reconnects with her husband, who, man or woman, is her "heart." I cried at those words, as did Ellen.

"I've found there are three things you can't change," she says. "First and second, the hormones don't affect the hair on your face or the voice. That's what the doctors all know. But recently I've added a third: it doesn't change the love you feel for people. It's like being in love with someone and being forced to separate from them, or you're pushing them away from you but you still love them just as much. The first time I saw couples on TV and one was a transsexual, and they'd stayed together, I thought it was so strange, I couldn't understand it. Now I can. It has something to do with the companionship between the two people you were, who aren't all that different now.

"It couldn't have worked with Eleanor, I understand that. But it's a sad thing. If two people get divorced, usually one wants it more than the other, but this is a case where people get divorced and both feel bad about it."

At some point we take a brief vacation together in southern Florida. As I'm puttering around, a thought flashes through my mind: how rarely I think about Ellen's transsexualism, other than an occasional pinprick of annoyance at a "T" moment.

For instance, once again she's wearing "exercise shorts," but there are no gyms or walking paths or beaches in the vicinity. She would say I'm looking through urban eyes at a phenomenon that is ubiquitous and suburban; I would say I've been to malls and nobody wears shorts that brief. In my view they're not age-appropriate, but her concept of age is clearly different from mine. I am chronologically "an older person" but think of myself as late middle age. She is chronologically an older person as well but thinks of herself as very young middle age. She disputes the idea of dressing for age: one should dress in whatever looks good. She wants to be an eye-catching female because she never had the chance, whereas I had my moment in the sun of romance and am relieved to be out of it.

It could be that I'm jealous of her youthfulness, hair that always looks better than mine, but I don't think so. For me, one of the compensatory benefits of aging is to be released from the tyranny of the mirror. It's as if whole sections of my brain, once dedicated to clothes, hair, makeup, the business of sexual attraction, are now free to turn to more essential matters, an emphasis on work made urgent by a sense of mortality.

What continues to disturb me most is the attempt by Ellen and other transsexuals to cheat time by going back to the future. Of course, modern life is full of such attempts: scientists trying to extend life indefinitely, women freezing their eggs for pregnancy at a later, more convenient time. But it's weird to feel, sometimes, as if I have a teenage sister when at other times we're two old ladies laughing at geriatric problems, transitioning, perhaps, into a "postgender" relationship.

When we walk down the sidewalk or into a restaurant, I no longer worry about onlookers, no longer give sidelong glances, checking for quizzical or amused expressions. Nor do I hear her always-problematic voice the way others seem to. I'm not sure why it is, but I seem deaf to the variations in Ellen's voice, say between "masculine low," "intersex low," "Lauren Bacall low," and "almost female." It's just a voice that is part Chevey, part Ellen, and I suppose that is what she will always be to me.

Ellen comes to New York in May 2012 to stay at her time-share on West Fifty-Sixth Street. Once again, a well-timed visit, as Andrew has a fall on May 14, the day before he's meant to go to the American Academy of Arts and Letters to be presented with a lifetime achievement award for criticism. There will be an exhibition of award winners' work, a celebrity-filled lunch, followed by an extended prize-giving ceremony. For weeks, we've been planning for the occasion, worrying (me, anyway) about him sitting on the stage for three hours. Now he's fractured his hip and has to have surgery at Mt. Sinai Hospital, the very day of the ceremony.

In yet another fortuitous arrival, it's while Andrew's in rehab at Mt. Sinai that Ellen comes up. A year ago she'd made a reservation for us to go on a dinner cruise around Manhattan, so I pick her up in a taxi and we go to Pier 61, where we board the *Bateaux*, a French boat enclosed in a dome of glass. We make our way to the tip of Manhattan and the view of Wall Street is staggering, the great monoliths of capitalism all lit up—or could they be the Stonehenge of a dying civilization? The dinner is fine, but there are too many people of all ages celebrating something or other, becoming joyfully inebriated, while the band amps up the decibel level just to keep pace. It's hard to talk, but I look at Ellen across the table and feel proud. The hair is less blond, and the lipstick seems to suit her. She looks very pretty, in dark pants and a cherry red jacket. This summer colors are in! Ellen is à la mode.

A thirtyish woman in a young trio sitting next to us, very attractive, says to me when we stand up for something, "You must be sisters!" Ellen is delighted when I tell her. But later, after disembarking, when Ellen's group from the Manhattan Club is waiting for a van, a man who's tipsy begins quizzing us in a friendly if repetitious way. Where are you girls from? Whatever we say, he says, "Thank God for that!" Later in the conversation, I think, but am not sure, that he refers to Ellen as "he." Seconds later, she leans over and asks me, "Did he say 'he'?" We're both unsure. And I wonder how it makes her feel. She smiles, she expects it, she carries it off with aplomb, but it must cut her up a bit as well. Each compliment a confidence builder, each "reading" a deflation. And a reminder of the dangers that are never far from her mind. She's not a fearful person, yet her life, easier now by far, is still hedged in by a need for caution.

A friend asks me if she's gotten sufficiently used to being a woman that the gestures have become second nature—does she have to stop and think about how she moves, sits, etc.? When I relay the question,

Ellen reports that the feminine mannerisms she had as a man and was always trying to suppress have become second nature to her now. "And after six years of practice," she says, "I hope I give the subliminal impression that I'm a woman, not a 'man in a dress.' Then there are a few mannerisms I turn on and off as the need arises. For example, most of my life I observed the way women walk and I learned (and still see it constantly) that women in general don't walk 'like a woman' or, for that matter, exhibit very many of the mannerisms we normally think of as feminine. It's also hard to walk that way for any distance, and since I walk considerable distances regularly, I relax my style to what may be a mixture of a masculine/feminine gait. It probably changes according to where I am, who I'm with." (The voice, too, seems to follow this pattern.)

"Some days I just can't believe what I went through—all those hospitalizations, surgeries, and electrolysis treatments. It's as if I were possessed."

Andrew is moved from Mt. Sinai to the Jewish Home, a subacute facility on the West Side. But the future looks bleak. He is very weak from the hip surgery and will probably need a wheelchair when he comes home. He will probably also require round-the-clock care, which in turn will probably necessitate my moving out of the bedroom. Our life together, already unalterably changed and (by me) grieved over, will become vastly worse from every point of view.

On Monday evening when I go to visit, he lights up as he always does. Pam, a private caretaker, is with him and when I see some food on his plate—he's always had a robust appetite—I'm surprised. Pam smiles. "That's his second dinner." But the very next day, Pam calls and says he became violently ill during physical therapy, a "bug," we

assume. I go to see him, get in bed with him. He can't hold anything
down. His stomach is very distended, like he has an obstruction. He
cries out when they poke it, but otherwise seems peaceful.

I go home, watch a DVD and a movie on television, call the floor
nurse at 9:30 P.M., and ask if I should be concerned. They reply in the
negative. Then at 3:30 in the morning on Wednesday, I get a call from
the nurse on duty. He's having trouble breathing, and they want to put
an IV in his neck. No, I say. Then the nurse says, You'd better get up
here, he could go in the next half hour.

I throw on some clothes and rush to the street. When I'm in a taxi,
I call Andrew's doctor, a physician in the palliative care center at Mt.
Sinai. He agrees, Don't let them do anything. Then I call the rehab
facility. He's not here, they report. He's been transferred to the emergency room at St. Luke's Roosevelt, on 114th Street and Amsterdam.
When I find him, he has only the oxygen mask over his nose. I tell him
I watched *Rear Window* earlier in the evening. He smiles and says
something that I can't make out. Those are his last words. I sit with
him as his breathing gets slower, slower. Five hours later, he dies.

It's Wednesday, June 20, 2012. On my cell phone, I call Ellen. She
wants to come up. I tell her not to, as I delusionally think I'll make ar-
rangements for Andrew's cremation and then get back to work. For
now I have people looking after me and want to save Ellen for later,
when the whole thing hits home. That's when I'll need some consolation. But twenty-four hours later I realize (or my friends make me realize) I need to have people over, and by then it's too late for her to come.

On that brilliantly sunny Sunday, as people arrive bearing flowers
and food, warmth and support, I realize the need for ritual as an expression of common bereavement. I regret Ellen not being here. I want
her to meet more of my friends.

Never mind—she'll come up for the memorial service in the fall.

· · · · · · ·

It's now October, seven years to the month from the last time I saw Chevey as my brother, the visit on which he broke the news. The memorial service I'm planning will be an elaborate affair—film clips from the movies Andrew loved, interspersed with friends and colleagues speaking about him. It'll take place at the Walter Reade Theater at Lincoln Center, with a reception afterward in the adjacent gallery. It's taken weeks of planning with my young cinephile filmmaking team. I'm anxious about it all, of course, but glad Ellen will be coming, and especially glad the two ex-wives will come as well. Beth will come up several days ahead and take us all out for dinner the night before the service. Eleanor will stay with Jeanne and be on call. Ellen knows enough people to be comfortable—still, there are many who are aware of the situation but haven't seen her yet. Will they ogle? Will she stand out in the crowd? Will all attention be focused on her? Will I care?

One night I dream that she's come to town and I've gone to meet her at the hotel where she's staying. (In real life she will stay with me.) I'm in the lobby waiting when she appears . . . but as Chevey! In coat and tie, smiling sheepishly. I understand she's left Ellen behind for a few days and come up as my brother. My sense in the dream is that it hurts her, that it's a sacrifice, and I feel terrible. But when I wake up, I forgive myself. In our unconscious, past and present meet, fantasy cohabits with reality, and wanting my brother doesn't mean that I want my sister less.

The memorial service goes off beautifully, as does the reception, or at least as far as I can see. Ellen hasn't brought a warm jacket so I've lent her one of mine—black wool, designer resale—and she looks terrific. My cousin Preston meets her for the first time, but another relative can't bring herself to approach. People tell me she's beautiful.

"Elegant" is a word I hear. And that she looks like me. I remind myself of my friend Ethel's warning as to what they *really* think, but find that I'm long past worrying, at least on my own behalf.

Afterward friends call. My agents, husband and wife, both think she's lovely. "She's charming," Georges says, "but like a woman, not a man."

A friend reports that another "good" friend, tipsy no doubt, kept going up to people, giggling and saying, "Tee-hee, have you seen Molly's 'sister'?"

My own opinion is that she carried the whole thing off with great poise. There were, however, a few glitches. Eleanor and Ellen are at my apartment the next day to console and help me. We are reviewing the previous evening and Eleanor has a bone to pick.

"Ellen, you introduced me to someone as your ex-wife. You can't do that. They'll think we're lesbians."

"Oh," says Ellen, to whom the thought hadn't occurred. "Next time I'll introduce you as my friend." That seems to satisfy Eleanor, but of course it's not right either. Once again we've landed awkwardly in a linguistic no-man's-land.

During the day, Ellen fixes things in the apartment—the telephone, a light—and answers some business questions. She and Eleanor open jars and pill bottles. I'm more helpless than usual, as my arm's in a cast from a fractured wrist—overexcitement on a quick trip to Paris before the memorial service. I'd thought I was walking on air rather than the cobblestones alongside the café Les Deux Magots. Looking everywhere but down, trying to swallow the whole city in one gulp after a long absence, I tripped over one of those heavy chains draped across the sidewalk to keep cars in their place.

Ellen and Eleanor want to help me organize my life, so we begin with the coat closet. Some of the coats, hats, and gloves are Andrew's;

most are mine. We start a box for the Salvation Army and implement a filing system: long coats on the left, short ones on the right; summer hats on the unreachable shelf, winter ones nestled into each other like Russian dolls; gloves, scarves, in perfect order. How long will it stay this way? Will the red rain hat and the neon-green and blue scarf, now in the box, find their way back into my closet after they're gone?

Ellen is about to start on a systematic rearrangement of my kitchen drawers when Eleanor says to her, "Just because you've thought and thought about these things, and have found the most efficient way to do everything, doesn't mean it's the right way for everybody." Ellen closes the drawer.

At dinner, as we make our way through several bottles of wine, we toast Andrew and reminisce. We are like three people at a train station, on our way somewhere, but with no signposts, no clear idea where we are going, and no grand arches overhead like those of Broad Street Station, where Mother, Chevey, and I once said our good-byes. It's just a whistle-stop platform in the middle of nowhere under miles of open sky. I'm now a widow; my brother is my sister; and Eleanor is an ex-wife, trying to move forward while stuck in a melancholy that won't let go. But if the intense happiness of being together on this night is inflected with ambiguity, full of uncertainty, and edged with sadness and loss, we are not forlorn. We don't feel abandoned, nor do we wish to turn away from each other. We are together on our separate journeys.

Acknowledgments

So many friends lent their encouragement and sympathy throughout the writing of this book—and also posed questions that mightn't have occurred to me—that I must simply thank you collectively. My deepest gratitude to my two sisters-in-law for understanding my need to write a book that promised to be an unwelcome intrusion in their lives. Georges and Anne Borchardt remain cherished longtime friends as well as agents. And I thank Kathryn Court and Ben George, my gifted editors.

Finally my debt to those persons and institutions without whose support and sanctuary there never would have been a book: the Virginia Center for the Creative Arts, the Guggenhcim Foundation, Donald Pels, and the New York Society Library.